Mark: My Words
Encounters With Jesus

MATT GORDON

CARRIAGE HOUSE PUBLISHERS

Mark: My Words–Encounters With Jesus
Copyright © 2022 by Matt Gordon

All scriptures are taken from the Holy Bible, New International Version®, NIV® Copyright © 1973, 1978, 1984, 2011 by Biblica, Inc.® Used by permission. All rights reserved worldwide.

Published by Carriage House Publishers

Library of Congress Control Number: 2022920892
Paperback ISBN: 979-8-9857824-6-2
eBook ISBN: 979-8-9857824-7-9
Cover design by Farrukh Khan
Interior page design: Carolyn Preul
Editing: Carriage House Publishers
Printed in the United States of America

Acknowledgment:
Special thanks to Katherine Burt, a fellow traveler and forever teacher.

Carriage
House
PUBLISHERS

SDG

CONTENTS

INTRODUCTION

For all the talk about faith, there sure isn't a whole lot of talk about, you know, faith. Imagine I send you an email invite with the subject line: Golf. You show up because you like free breakfast. We sit down and proceed to engage for 45 minutes, never even teeing up the topic of golf. It would probably be a tad confusing for you. Worse yet would be if I actually did talk about golf because, in truth, I don't care about it, play it, and my knowledge of the game is fairly … wait for it … subpar. (Sorry.)

This is how it goes with faith—especially, Christianity. We do a whole lot of talking around the thing. We mention it in passing, crochet tenets of it on pillows, and even make a show to pray before meals at holidays when we want to impress the out-of-town family members with our piety. But we don't actually talk about it all that much, and certainly not all that directly.

Take church. Now maybe your church does go straight for it. Maybe it marches around in Jesus' shadow, hopscotching in his footsteps. That's great. You can return this book.

For the rest of us, the church gathering is like that workmate who you discover is also visiting the branch office tomorrow. "Hey, want to carpool?" she asks.

No, Sheila, I don't. I don't know you and I think I'd rather listen to good music than spend two hours in a car with someone who could be a murderer for all I know, I answer. In my head.

Out loud I say, "You bet, girl! Oooo, this is gonna be fun!" I say it all sassy. Like we are in a sorority together or something. It is a sad, sassy display. Sadder still is how I fret about it all night. *What are we going to talk about for two hours!?*

Anxiety sets in. A fear of the dreaded silences. The boredom—what if she is a cat person and insists on telling me all about her formidable litter (in both senses of the word)?

Usually, this whole scenario is borderline terrible. But sometimes I take my place in Sheila's minivan (she had it when her kids were little and, *by golly*—her words, not mine—*just couldn't go back*). We hit the open road, and she says, "This baseball trade market is fierce. You think the Cardinals are going to make a splash?" or "What's your overall impression of the cinematic choices of *The Office?*" or "What do you think Shakespeare was like as a person?" or "Waterslides: go …"

Sheila says any of this and my heart answers, "Let's go!" We may get to the office and keep driving West. Chase a sunset together or something.

There is nothing like a great conversation focused on something you really care about. My wife understands this. I've been late coming home before and my apology goes like this: "I'm so sorry. He brought up Huhot strategies right when we were finishing up our meeting."

"Well, I know that is a love language of yours …" she replies.

Yet I attend the weekly church gathering—the one time all week the body gets together—and I cringe like I'm getting into Shelia's van for the first time. Someone who looks like an Express mannequin come-to-life hops up on stage and talks politics for 40 minutes. Or social issues. *Yes! I was hoping I'd get to resolve a hyper complex, nuanced issue by hearing precisely and absolutely how God views things, and even how He would vote! Boy, am I glad I came here today for a dose of politicization and didn't watch the same political*

coverage from the 76 cable stations doing the exact same thing this morning.
No, this is better because it is coming from a pastor. My pastor. My politically
informed pastor. Praise be!

Or sometimes I show up for the church gathering and a TED talk breaks
out. Well, sort of. Usually TED talks feature experts in a niche field
delivering their one home run talk on a subject they've spent decades
studying, learning, and applying. So this is a TED talk but, you know, sort
of worse. Less informed. And judgier. *Cool. Glad I brought a friend!*

Often one shows up to church and we sort of talk about nothing. I visited
some elderly folks recently in what was supposed to be a 30-minute
meeting. Three-and-a-half hours later, I drove home and tried to chronicle
what we had discussed. It was easier to come up with the handful of things
we didn't talk about. And honestly, though we covered the entire Twentieth
Century, there wasn't any depth. Any substance. We were just sort of taking
turns saying things. It was like spin-the-bottle with random speech taking
the place of kissing. Church is sometimes just someone taking a pretty long
turn saying things.

It is weird. We gather up to share a common interest together, maybe
inviting outsiders to observe this common interest with us, and then we
don't really talk about it.

Imagine a salesperson coming to your door and telling you about a
revolutionary product that would absolutely change your life. You lean in,
listening, hoping for that chance to take the time machine and invest in
Apple. And then the salesperson starts talking about baseball or something.

Or the Mormon boys. Maybe girls do it now too—I can't say I know. But
what I do know is that we moved to a neighborhood once where all the
houses had NO SOLICITING stickers on the doors. I thought this was
strange and unwelcoming and didn't know why until the doorbell rang.
Two well-dressed boys stood at my door. We had finished bringing the final

moving box in about 18 seconds prior. Apparently, our neighborhood was on Salt Lake City's radar as a high-level target.

I never minded. In fact, I liked talking to the Mormon missionaries when they'd swing by. I'd have them in, we'd have some non-alcoholic drinks. It was nice. What I really liked is that they never even tried to give me seven leadership strategies to reshape my life. They didn't tell me how to vote. No, those homeboys took me straight to Utah. They were dropping Jesus Christs and Brigham Youngs and Joseph Smiths like they were paid for each use of certain catchwords. You gonna ride your bicycle in 200-degree heat, park in my lawn, barge past the NO SOLICITING warning, then yeah, let's go! Do what you came to do—mission out and all that.

"We need to talk"—you ever say that? Usually what follows is serious, somber, important. What follows that phrase is usually change, termination, a break-up, a diagnosis. Bad news.

I recall having to track down someone once and use these words. I rang the bell like a Mormon boy and waited. The door swung open and I didn't know what else to say—how to begin. I was preparing to deliver the news that this person's father had died. "We need to talk ..." was the beginning before we came to the sad end.

I'll repeat those words again, that we need to talk about faith. About Christianity. The church needs to quit trying to be culturally relevant at the cost of being culturally useful, and get to the point. Or, more directly, we need to get to the *person*. And, no, not the person in the audience. Perhaps there is a time to talk vision and mission and leadership and finances and planning— sure. But we get these small windows, minute opportunities. And what we do with those moments says much. What we choose to talk about won't define us because it already has. Our loves bubble to the surface.

I wonder if Jesus could mosey up to the stage or carpool with us to the branch office, what he might say? If he had 30 minutes for a quick chat?

"Brothers and sisters, we need to be more active civically because there are some issues on the upcoming ballot that pose a real threat to the Kingdom I'm trying to build."

"Dearly beloved, sin and eternity … can wait because I have seven strategies for servant leadership to share!"

"Did you all see the game last night? My Dad, was it something!"

No. I don't think he'd say any of that.

If Jesus had 30 minutes with us, as he often does with people he encounters in scripture, he'd talk about God and how we can be right with God through him. He'd talk about faith, but not as an abstract. As an action. As a way of life. As a worthwhile, difficult pursuit. Humbly, he'd talk about himself.

Other stuff matters—even baseball, kind of—but if what is at the heart of a local church is not the person and work of Christ, then we will have a wobbly foundation based on an ill-chosen cornerstone. If the church is not built upon Christ, then what are we even trying to build? The Bible— *shocker!*—claims that Christ is the cornerstone to the church. And then if we define church, I think we could biblically say it is the collection of believers. That collection, like any collection, is made up of individuals. By proxy, then, if what is at the heart of a Christian is not the person and work of Christ, then, again, we will have a wobbly foundation based on an ill-chosen cornerstone. It begs the question: What are we even doing?

And this is what has led me to seek answers in the *Gospel of Mark.*

First, it, like this point, is short. Who doesn't like checking out an audiobook and seeing: *Time to Read—Five Hours.* Turn that baby up to 3x speed and you and Shelia can knock it out on the drive to the branch office.

Second, it is a firsthand account of Jesus. If I want to talk or consider faith, then it is good to go to the source. I don't want to hear what you have to say about the Koran—I want to put hands on the thing and read it. And if Christianity is my interest, my faith, and my pursuit, what I crochet into pillows, then I'd better frequently be putting eyes on Christ. In Mark, we are likely reading Peter's account of his dear friend Jesus. I can picture Peter in some ancient-world Airbnb pacing and rattling off stories, while Mark hurriedly scribbled down the torrent of words.

And because it is sourced from Peter, it is direct. My son's teeth were all jacked up early in life because his fingers were constantly in there. Peter probably had ancient-world braces thanks to all the time his foot spent in his mouth. The guy just went for it. This gospel captures that, as it is loaded with fast-paced action. I pretend to like Wes Anderson movies because it makes me feel better than you. But sometimes, and it pains me to admit it, you just need Michael Bay blowing stuff up in your life. The *Gospel of Mark* is a dramatic high-speed chase. Only instead of chasing down a bad guy while there is still time, we are in a frenetic pursuit of the ultimate good guy (or perhaps he is in pursuit of us).

Whichever view we take, in this gospel, we see Jesus. His life. His work. The *Gospel of Mark* is a bunch of quick cuts told with rabid excitement and urgency. In fact, *immediately* is one of the most used words of the book, repeated over 40 times in most translations. It reminds me of the guy you sit next to on the plane. Before you can buckle in, he starts in about his life or his business or his hobby. You need a stiff drink before the crew can even tell you what to do in the event of an emergency. Putting on his oxygen mask before your own wasn't even in the cards in this case. But then something happens in flight. His overwhelming passion and authenticity, well, it wins you. By the time the plane lands, you are ready to sign up for the cult. *I get it! I'm in!*

Peter via Mark is pumped. And what has him so excited?

Well, stay seated until the captain turns off the fasten seatbelt sign.

1. NEWS

On a rainy Wednesday morning, my young sons were outside testing their umbrellas. I'm sure the neighbors were judging our parenting as our tiny children danced and splashed and played lightsabers in the rainy driveway at 7 a.m. I called to my sons from the garage, and they ignored me. That's pretty much how we roll in *mi casa*. I tried again more firmly, adding gravel to the dulcet tones, to no avail. And then I hit them with, "Hey, we need to talk!"

They moped in slowly, dripping wet and expecting the worst.

"We need to talk, guys," I repeated. They looked at each other, making a silent truce not to betray one another—a vow they would surely break at the first mention of timeout. "Listen, Dada is taking off work today and heading down to the Cardinals game. Would you all be willing to go with me?"

Bedlam ensued. They sprinted back to the rainy delirium, only this time they left a galaxy far, far away and their umbrellas behind, opting instead for maniacal imaginary homeruns.

We come to Mark with the rainy history of the world hanging in the balance. There had been hardship, struggle, murder, distrust, slavery, exodus, sojourning, captivity, war, deceit. But maybe the worst of it had come to pass last: silence. Not some awkward blip before someone starts talking about the weather either. No, we are talking silence. After a redemptive history of an ever-present forgiving God showing up when things are bleakest, the prophets were muted. No words came; no books written; no stories proclaimed. For 400 years.[1]

And then in Mark 1:4, a voice cries out in the wilderness. John the Baptist grabs the dormant mic and, in some ways, speaking for God, spits ala Jay-Z, "Allow me to reintroduce myself."[2] He speaks of repentance and the forgiveness of sins. He speaks of good news.

It is me in that garage, taking my underserving children aside, saying, "We need to talk," and then zigging where expectations were zagging. They expected trouble—the worst. They got good news.

This is what has Peter so excited: "The beginning of the good news about Jesus the Messiah."[3] It has been 400 years, and now we are hearing something. Surely this isn't good. Surely we are in big, big trouble. Surely all that silence was a harbinger of heartache. And then, BAM, good news—the best news.

For my boys that day, the news was good but only because of the promise to come. A day away to eat sugary, expensive food and ignore baseball (and dad's steady refrains to sit still). John the Baptist is saying some different things in a different way, but it doesn't mean much … *unless*. Unless the promise is delivered. All the build-up in the world amounts to nothing if the band doesn't take the stage, if the rain washes out the promised game to come.

And then Jesus takes the field: "At that time Jesus came from Nazareth in Galilee and was baptized by John in the Jordan."[4]

The hype man delivered. With the silence had come a darkness, and God's eventual answer is the light of the world. John had promised and God had delivered.

I wonder what I hype? We all do it. I was watching a show on Netflix with my wife, and I checked out the reviews on IMDb. One episode, at that time, had over 22,000 user reviews. People telling me it is utter garbage and people telling me it is the nectar of existence. All of them, unpaid, leaving their thoughts, selling unknown masses on an idea—to watch or not to watch. And we all do it. All the time. We share our loves (and hates). We recommend. We are walking billboards for politicians, pastors, producers. I'm pretty sure that we are supposed to strive to be like Jesus in this world, and I'm even more certain that we are going to mostly fail. He had that whole fully-God thing going for him after all. But I'm also pretty sure that we are supposed to strive to be like John the Baptist, and I'm even more certain that when we point people to Jesus and let him write the checks, it cashes. It works. And it is good. Of all the things in the world I hype, is hope among them?

Jesus is baptized by John. What a strange scene. Think John had any imposter syndrome going on? He had been telling his followers someone greater was coming. Then that greater person shows up and John is probably like, "See! Told you!" Then to Jesus, "Levitate or something. Show them!"

And Jesus responds, "Would you please baptize me?"

Had to be confusing for John and his followers. Humility is always just a little confusing, isn't it?

But the real magic of the scene is in the breakthrough. Jesus is breaking through the water—a picture of so many things: the Israelites breaking through the Red Sea to freedom; the sound and light breaking through the silence and darkness. Perhaps, the most wonderful picture, though, is that of the new creation breaking through into the old. We see this through the presence of Jesus being joined by the Holy Spirit and God the Father. All three persons of the Trinity showing up and showing out, as with the original creation, now with the new creation. The Spirit, in this scene, descends on Jesus like a dove. I'm not sure what that even means, but I know way back in Genesis, at the original creation scene, "Now the earth was formless and empty, darkness was over the surface of the deep, and the Spirit of God was hovering over the waters."[5] A word that can be substituted in both scenes is *fluttering*—the same verb and action used for the same purpose: the act of making things new.[6]

Following that Genesis verse comes this one, "And God said, 'Let there be light,' and there was light."[7] And here in Mark, God, looking down on the light of the world, speaks: "You are my Son, whom I love; with you I am well pleased."[8] Pleased like God was with creation.

Something is happening.

Now, this all could be made up. And if so, kudos to Mark and Peter for baking up such a deliciously creative plot. I mean this is some next level storytelling—J.K. Rowling is in the corner blushing at this point. Harry Potter's a muggle compared to this magic.

But if it isn't made up and this fisherman and his friend weren't next-level storytelling masterminds, something is happening. The crowd looking on had to feel it. And it probably felt a lot like fear. If this did happen, we have the Trinity present here on earth. God, in fullness, present.

Then the scene ends and Jesus shoots out of the Jordan like a cannonball. Healing. Leading. Speaking. And what does he say?

Well, it isn't leadership lessons or talks on politics. In verse 14, we get a glimpse of his message, of the words with which he chooses to break the silence: "'The time has come,' he said. 'The kingdom of God has come near. Repent and believe the good news!'"

The good news. Mark opens the book with it. Jesus opens his ministry with it. Heaven opens its doors with it. The good news.

Jesus didn't come to give a series of talks. He came to live a life. One that claimed the answer. Not the answer to how to be a more dynamic church or cuss less or have more money. That is us cheapening the news. The good news is that the presence of God, of all goodness forever, is available to us. To any of us. That our shame and our fear and our doubt doesn't have to define us. That silence doesn't have to win. That darkness dissipates with light. That hope for all awaits the *all*. In Mark, Jesus is calling. Waiting. Ready.

Are we?

After I delivered the good news, we drove down to the ballpark, my boys and I. Along the way, the rain stopped.

2. FRIENDS

In 1916, a young man trudged off to war, claiming that leaving his wife was, "Like a death."[9] Heady play, that. He knew she'd read that. Imagine if he said something like, "It'll be a nice little reset" or "Distance makes the heart grow fonder." No, he nailed it with "like a death." I tried it with my wife the other day when leaving for work and didn't get quite the fanfare I hoped for (which was sex). Just a modest eyeroll is all. You have to start somewhere, I guess.

What follows death is afterlife, so if leaving home and wife were the death, the afterlife was Hell, for what other way can one describe war? War alone is an absurdity. Think of it: I line up some of my people and you line up some of yours. I kill yours and you kill mine until one of us has had enough or there is no more left of either. All this destructive conflict over money, power, or position. War is absurd.

Even so, the First World War attempted to outpace all the wars that came before it in its gruesomeness. Trench warfare was a macabre fecklessness, like a tired game of whack-a-mole, only the moles were humans: bone, sinew, head, heart.

Since a soldier couldn't go *up* without risking a bullet to the brain, the men hunkered *down*—into the muck and mire. Disease. Stench. Rats the size of small dogs.

Amid this darkness, the homesick second lieutenant was surprised by light.

In this twisted setting, he observed a courage that unified schoolteachers and lawyers and plumbers. Knit together in the crucible of shared suffering, they forged friendships far deeper than the trenches they occupied.

When he returned home, the second lieutenant sought to keep that alive. He began meeting with a small group of men to talk politics, war, culture, books, family, and all that lies beyond.

One meeting, in particular, stands out. Not because it culminated with a walk in the woods—this was somewhat common, apparently. And it wasn't just that two or three of the men stayed together after the walk—the return to the dangerous combination of warm fire and strong beer likely fueled this proverbial flame. With flame in hearth and brew in hand, the former second lieutenant shared some good news with his questioning atheist friend. This is what made this encounter distinct, even remarkable. These two men had entered the evening with much in common, but they left with one more thing: a common faith. This faith and friendship would shape a generation and has impacted you in some way, as it has just about everyone else too.[10]

These men were named J.R.R. Tolkien and C.S. Lewis. After this fireside encounter, the two remained good friends, and each credited the other, in some way, for inspiring the completion of their respective masterworks, *The Lord of the Rings* and *The Chronicles of Narnia*.[11] Present in both collections is an idea they fortified in war and brought home. It is this old, forgotten thing called friendship.

I'm a big LOTR fan. These days, grandparents aren't called "grandpa" and "grandma." No, you have to be Gaga or Nuno or Poppop or Cricket. (Yes, I knew a woman who desired that moniker once.) Before my time, I went ahead and picked my own name based on my LOTR fandom and my favorite character, the wizard Gandalf. My future grandchildren will lovingly and reverently refer to me as Grandalf the Gray. *Cool, right!?*

Right?

I'm not sure, though, how I would feel about Gandalf if he were alone. Nor any of the characters really. It is their togetherness that draws me. The first part of the book is titled, *The Fellowship of the Ring*. Fellowship: a group bound. Bonded together in common cause. There is something so powerful about that.

At the heart of this fellowship is a pair of friends named Frodo and Sam. When reading the book, their friendship comes off as stalwart, steady, and fetching. But then the movies came out. Peter Jackson really stuck close to the source material, *God bless him*. And on screen, this male-with-male tenderness, full of vulnerability and affection, well, was odd. The two men were in love, in a technical sense, and it didn't seem to jibe with male-with-male relationships across most of our culture.

Cue the memes! That is what happened: the scenes of Sam and Frodo showing emotional intimacy began to be highlighted in memes depicting their relationship as homoerotic.[12] Because that is what we do—who we've been since the 60's (1960's or maybe like 1960 BCE—nothing new under the sun, yeah?).[13] We gravitate toward the sexual. We find and favor romantic love.

Take gossip magazines. How many front-page stories do you see, as you peruse these rags in line at the grocery store, about a couple of Hollywood friends playing pickleball? Or talking deeply? No, the headlines are about hook-ups and break-ups, not hang-outs.

Or consider songs. Think of your favorite love song. Now ask the 15 people you gave this book to—subtle sales plug there; always be closing!—and you'll find 15 different answers. Now do the same thing with songs about friendship. You'll find you all either went the *Toy Story* route or have friends in low places. Because that is about it. (Outside-Looking-In: James Taylor). There are so many more songs about romantic love.

How about shows? Every show of the last 25 years pretty much has to have a love interest, regardless of genre. Even the fact that I say "love interest" and our minds all go to romantic love betrays our sensibilities. Comedies dabble in romance. Shows about monsters have to underline characters' sexual interests and appetites. Even the aptly titled show *Friends* finds four of the six comrades entering into romantic relationships with one another; only the two oddballs stay true to the title.

We obsess over romantic love. A close second? Familial love. Show of hands: How many people reading this sentence have been to a marriage conference? (Okay, put your hand down—you look ridiculous.) How many have been to a friendship conference? Huh. No takers. Think of parenting classes and endless books on raising kids. Even the leftover sitcoms attest: *Modern Family*, *Married with Children*, *Family Matters*, etc.

None of this is pointed out with judgment, mind you. Let's use the postmodern maxim: *It is what it is.* Followed by its younger sibling: *just sayin'.* Our passions and obsessions reveal our value basis. And this value basis hints at how foreign the idea and practice of good friendship is to us. Yet friendship is vitally important to our experience and our faith.

Mark 2 captures both.

We see Jesus entering Capernaum, the place that had become his homebase of operations. This is evident because he is there, but so is everyone else. They follow him—he is known, and where to find him is too. Jesus goes to a house and so does the crowd. By verse 3, we see what kind of parties Jesus threw—they were BYOB: Bring Your Own Bodies. Some men came carrying a pallet with a paralyzed guy on it.

Then, audaciously, since they can't get through the crowd, they tote this dude up on the roof and begin making an opening. Homes in this time and region tended to have roof access, sort of where the barbecue grill and some sun chairs were kept. So, there was probably an opening of sorts, but it wasn't accessible from the outside, so these guys had to dig around to remove the compartment leading into the house. Or, perhaps, that house didn't come with roof access, in which case they had to remove the layers of dirt and clay and palm fronds to gain access. Whatever the case, we have some digging, some trespassing, and some good old-fashioned vandalism going on. Which tells me that this is a little bonkers, okay?[14]

What we witness here is reckless love. Unstoppable affection. Persevering camaraderie. These are friends. Full stop. And friendship is different; it just is.

It isn't, for starters, just based on biology. It isn't a relationship based on a desire to procreate or for help in surviving. I would contend that friendship is necessary for thriving, however.

Proverbs 17:17 says, "A friend loves at all times, and a brother is born for a time of adversity." That saying can be taken with a touch of compare-and-contrast. A sibling, we can infer, is stuck with us and we are stuck with them. A friend is different because a friend is chosen. The friend doesn't have to be there. Their obligation is non-obligatory, so when they show up, when they load you up on a pallet, when they barge through a roof for you—well, it is because they *choose* to love you. There is a beauty in not picking our family (and them not picking us), in that we learn to love people we wouldn't necessarily choose. Friends, though, are chosen. My family will bury me someday, and it is my friends who will attend the wake.

Many of us have two problems. First, we have a lack of friends. Second, our friends are poorly chosen.

There was some leadership quip that seemed to surface in the early 2000s. I don't who said it or what research they based it on, but it hit social media with a rage. Every employed person on earth then quoted it 17 times a day for approximately five years. Paraphrased, it went something like this: You become the average of the five people you hang out with the most.[15]

I think it caught on because it is pretty wise. It seems fairly true. It also is unoriginal by thousands of years.

Check out Proverbs 22:24-25: "Do not make friends with a hot-tempered person, do not associate with one easily angered, or you may learn their ways and get yourself ensnared." Or Proverbs 13:20: "Walk with the wise and become wise, for a companion of fools suffers harm." Some of us pick friends who juggle grenades and naively neglect the reality of shrapnel.

Proverbs 27:9 gives advice on selecting the five (or three or nine or whatever) people we shape our life with: "Perfume and incense bring joy to the heart, and the pleasantness of a friend springs from their heartfelt advice."

Pleasantness is sometimes translated as sweetness.[16] For me, sweetness brings to mind Sweet Tarts. I have a dozen in my mouth right now. I love sweet things, especially candy. Through this, I've determined dentist to be the vocation that most needs to implement a lie detection protocol. "Do you floss?" the hygienist always asks right out the gate.

"Yeppers," I lie through my rotting teeth.

Then she begins getting in there and flossing me and a whole Skittle pops out.

"Whoa, that's weird and unexpected!" I exclaim, popping the Skittle back into my mouth and finishing the job.

I love sweet things and I can go to Mr. Bulky's in the local mall and do work right now if I want. In the ancient world there weren't (gasp) Mr. Bulky's. Grocery stores didn't have those movie-style boxes of Lemonheads for 99 cents. Because there weren't grocery stores or movies or Lemonheads. In the ancient world you couldn't just go grab sweets; sweetness had to be sought. Found. Discovered. Then, for the work and effort, cherished. And that is how it is with friendship—it must be sought.

Found. Discovered. Cherished.

C.S. Lewis says friendship begins with a person saying to another, "What? You too? I thought I was the only one!"[17] The only one who air-drummed to that '90's break-up band. The only one who watched *Summer Heights High*. The only one who actually saved the whales. The only one who had that score on Tetris. The only one who felt that way.

This agrees with Aristotelian thought. In *Nicomachean Ethics*, Aristotle writes of a friendship ladder. At the bottom are friendships based on utility—"You scratch my back and I'll scratch yours." Then, up a wrung or two, comes friendship based on admiration—why the jocks group up in high school, or why you love hanging out with the friend who makes you laugh a lot. All the way up the ladder is Aristotle's "perfect friendship." These are relationships that bond based on some virtuous thing outside one another—a dream, a cause, a passion.

Lovers look longingly into each other's eyes. They talk about their relationship. "How are we doing? How's our relationship?" they say. Lovers don't ever want to hang up the phone, "You hang up first … no you … no you." I cannot fathom taking my friend Nate to lunch and asking what he thinks about *us*. Nor have we ever said goodbye to one another on the phone, much less argued over who does it first. And the reason isn't because we are a couple of muscled-up alphas stuck in toxic masculinity. I cry in *You've Got Mail*, okay? It is because friends don't look face-to-face. They stand side-by side and look out at the world, at problems, at issues, at challenges, at adventures.

Frodo trekked off to Mordor and so did Sam. Turns out they might as well go together. Their destination bound them, but so too did their love of home. They talked about the Shire and protecting and preserving it, of returning to it. "You love home too! I thought I was the only one," they repeated, a mantric revitalizing of relationship, of friendship.

The issue many of us have in finding friends is a lack of mission. Was it Thoreau who spoke of the mass of men leading lives of quiet desperation?[18] By the way, if you ever play a homemade style of charades with friends, the kind where you get to supply your own clues, this is a really good quote to throw in the bucket. Meryl Streep ain't getting a point trying to act out that quote. Thoreau was probably onto something. We have families and jobs. We watch some TV. Take a walk. Then, BOOM, we die. Okay, that might be a bit hyperbolic, but it doesn't feel like a stretch to say that many of us lack purpose. That our lives have become less and less missional. That as provision has become more and more plentiful for much of the world, that passion has been made scarce. We have forgotten what it is to live on mission.[19]

Younger children haven't. You take a kid to a playground. He sees a girl on the monkey bars. And that's enough. "You want to be my friend?" The equation is simple—*you like monkey bars, I like monkey bars, let's like monkey bars together. Let's be about that.*

We have forgotten how to make the mundane into mission—to push and dream and devote.

Which brings us, finally, back to faith. At the heart of every mission is faith. I don't work tirelessly training to fly a rocket that will blow up at launch. I have faith that it will launch, that it will work, and so do the people working alongside me—*Ad astra!* We strike off on the open road, assuming, despite challenges and setbacks, that we will arrive at a destination. We are forever a people of faith.

And faith itself is missional. Those with a faith in Christ are called to pursue goodness, to participate in the Kingdom of God, to grieve with those who grieve, to rejoice with those who rejoice, to love God and people. It is wrapped up in action, in mission.

Lewis spits truth when he speaks of "pathetic people" who want friends but can never find them.[20] It is because they are looking for the wrong thing. Find mission and you'll meet-cute with fellow travelers. Board a bus to Buffalo and, SURPRISE, you'll find others going to Buffalo. You'll ask each other existential why's concerning that destination, and you'll be yoked together on the basis of mission: *We, together, go! Onward to Buffalo!* Not quite William Wallace's "Freedom!" but it is made of the same stuff.

I've always enjoyed the books of Steinbeck and am amazed at how much story he packs into 98 pages in *Of Mice and Men*. In it we meet George— who is little, smart, and mean. And Lennie—who is big, dumb, and nice. These two dudes have no business in league with one another. Seemingly, they have little in common, and even their travelling together flummoxes the other characters in the story. (Because, as mentioned earlier, when it comes to friendship, we've lost our way.) As you read the tale, the connection becomes clearer and clearer. At anxious moments in the plot, Lennie looks to George and says, "Tell me about the rabbits, George."

George then enters a trance-like state—the beautiful dimension where life becomes poetry—and tells Lennie about the house they would build once they roll up a stake. They'd each have a room, plus a room for guests. They'd have a big front porch, and from it they'd be able to look out on their land and all they were growing.

"Tell me about the rabbits," Lennie would interrupt.

And George would tell his simple-minded friend about the rabbits Lennie would get to tend all by himself.[21]

George and Lennie were fellow travelers toward the dream of home. And the power of their mission overcame even their differences.

These days many are concerned about diversity, about becoming groups with less homogeny. And the goal of becoming more multi-ethnic and diverse is good. But I would say they aren't missions. Rather, they are the results of good mission. Like if I were to tell my Black brother-in-law, "Hey, Mario, you gotta come to my church."

I hope he'd say, "Why?"

One way or the other, my answer will illustrate my point. If my next line is, "Well, um, we are trying to become more diverse. More multi-ethnic." Why would he want to be part of that? I'm telling him that I need him to help *me* become better or feel better. I need him to complete me. I need him to ease my social conscious. I, I, I ... the crux of the ask is me. Him entering into *my* world to meet *my* need.

But if my next line is, "Man, we are chasing Christ. We are passionate. Lives are being changed." Then I'm inviting him to Buffalo or to the homestead we are building. I'm asking him to be bound to Mordor to destroy evil once and for all. We, we, we ... the crux of my ask is the Cross. It is *us* following Jesus up Mount Doom and returning to life eternal on the other side.

In the trenches, Tolkien witnessed unity, not because some general demanded it or gave a good sermon on it. He saw a bunch of men from different socio-economic positions, from different places, unified by the hope of staying alive. Their shared hope was the unifier, not unity itself. I love the Bonhoeffer quote that says the person who loves his idea of community will destroy it, but the person who loves his neighbor as himself will create community.[22]

Mission. It brings unity, diversity, and community, and it is the environmental necessity for good friendship.

And in that friendship, in those trenches, something else happens. I love how Proverbs 17 says a friend loves at all times. Blend that with Proverbs 25:17: "Seldom set foot in your neighbor's house. Too much of you, and they will hate you." What you get is a friend for all times but not *all* the time. Meaning a true friend sees and knows you. That sometimes you need to be alone and sometimes you need anything but. Sometimes you need a hug; other times, a drink. A friend knows you and you know them.

We all have utility-based relationships. The kind where you are very close to your workmates until you change workplaces. Your high school friends who fade with each passing year. The relationships that are incredible until your company flops or marriage dissolves. People come into our lives all the time who just want to cuddle up to our successes. Others swoop in because they are attracted to failure—who doesn't love a good fixer-upper?

Friendships are different. They don't love your successes. They don't love your failures. They love you *anyway*. All your anyways—they are right there with you.

Back to Mark and these men in the story. The paralyzed man is lowly. He had a challenge. You think of how we as a culture fail to love, serve, and honor those with disabilities. But in those times—in that culture—this man was made to crawl in the dirt because he was viewed as little better than dirt. Their infirm were barred from society. Outcasted. Othered. This man was lowly.

Because of that, he probably wasn't super fun. I think of these four men carrying him as being somewhat youthful since carrying him, climbing with him, and lowering him was pretty laborious in nature. I imagine them wanting to go chase the ladies at Club Capernaum and not being able to because the limitations of their friend. There are some things they just can't do when he is around.

Surely, he was a hassle. With this guy, you were the one bringing dinner to his house. He wasn't footing many bills, nor coming for a visit. He is that friend who never volunteers to drive times a hundred.

Yet.

Yet they show up at his house. They load him up. They carry him. All of this means they think of him and how Jesus might help him. They care. And they care because they love him. Without getting much worldly gain back, they love him. Understand, then, that this is not a natural love. Natural love loves because it makes sense. I love my boss because he is rich and can give me stuff—makes sense. I love athletes because they entertain. I love the life of the party because his or her own life gives life to me.

But supernatural love? Love that isn't paid back; love without earthly return? Well, that is the kind of love ascribed to God. That God is Love, and that Love loves us. We have nothing to offer God—nothing God needs at least. He isn't pining for my best joke or some stroke of genius from me ... *yet*. Yet while I was sinner, God loved me enough to give his life for me. When we love those in our lives this way, we are loving like God loves us.

These men have that kind of reckless, yet-love. They show up. They load him up. They go.

But then they do one better, and it is what any who read this line and believe in Jesus ought to realize. It is this: If Jesus is any kind of real to you, the best thing you can do for your friends is bring them to Jesus.

This is sort of how it works—how God set it up. That the good news and friendship are intimately woven. Pre-belief, it is our friends who carry us closer to God. For the disciples, it was a brother who followed first, a friend went before and then couldn't stop talking about Jesus, couldn't hide the transformation. After we begin walking in stride with Jesus, we look back and remember the gospel love our friends poured onto the soils of faith in our life. Paul's first mission after converting wasn't to write a bunch of letters or plant several churches. It was to go to the next city and meet a friend. Tolkien and Lewis were buddies first, then brothers.

This leads to two questions: *Who in your life are you bringing to Jesus?* and

Who in your life is bringing you to Jesus?

These men brought their paralytic friend to Jesus. Before they did, I wonder if he objected?

"Hey, guys. Where are we going? I sort of think I want to stay in today …"

"Okay, guys, big crowd ahead. Maybe we should call it …"

"Guys, what are we doing? Not sure if the roof is the best place for me …"

Maybe the roof part was the most comfortable for him? What, was he going to fall off and get *more* paralyzed? The questions probably started back up, though, when the digging did: "Guys, this seems pretty illegal. *Guys!?*"

Whatever the objections, they pressed on and lowered him down, down, down, into the crowd, before Jesus.

"When Jesus saw their faith … ," the Bible says.[23] Whoa! That is a big deal. It wasn't based on the paralyzed man's faith or lack of faith—it was the faith of his friends. Healing comes as a result of faith, but sometimes it is the faith of others. This is compelling isn't it? I wonder how many prayers my mother offered before I realized my own salvation? She was always there, lowering me before Jesus, showing her faith. Who do you hope for, pray for? Who do you stand resolutely for before they can stand for themselves? The upstart. The wayward. The sick. The strung out. There is that old song that says, "Be thou my vision." Well, we can be the vision for other people until they get eyes to see. Jesus tells someone that if you follow a blind guide, you fall into a pit. Wouldn't the inverse be just as true? Follow a guide with vision and you avoid the pitfalls long enough to find the fields of faith.

The healing Jesus gives because of this faith is first of a spiritual nature. "Your sins are forgiven," he says to the paralyzed man.

The scribes don't like that. They question this. Only God can forgive sins, they reason. Correctly. Their logic is actually good. Only God forgives sin. This guy is forgiving sins. This guy isn't God. Ergo, blasphemy! *Let's get him!* Like so many of us, they are missing a step. Like if a dude walks on water, it is impossible. The Bible shows a dude walking on water. Therefore, the Bible is impossible. *Hey, this is easy to sort out! The math of this world is tidy—no remainders!* Unless … unless the dude walks on water. Unless it is true. Unless what is normatively impossible happens. Because if that happens, well, you don't question the thing that is happening, but rather everything else. The math is different. It is like when math grows up and turns to algebra in eighth grade and you are like, *Hey! What happened to all the counting? I liked the counting!*

These religious leaders use their simple, safe logic like a shield to hide behind, sparing themselves from potential arrows of truth. Jesus knows their thoughts and answers their unbelief with a physical healing.

This is the big crescendo! "Get up. Take your mat and walk!"

The crescendo sounds to some like a sad trombone—to those limping along. Those still paralyzed. Those with chronic pain. It is easy to read this and think, *Well, why isn't everyone healed?* There are probably other paralytics ironically within walking distance, and they, while all this is going on, just lie there. Forever lie there. *Again, why isn't everyone healed!?*

My answer is this: they are. Everyone who seeks healing from Jesus is healed. Every. Time. That answer can seem irresponsible, especially when cancer comes calling, when the lingering power of a stroke won't relent.

But let's refresh things, shall we? This one time there was this guy named Jesus. He died. Then, supposedly, he came back to life. Now, everyone else dies and doesn't do that. They just stay dead. So basically, we have this one guy do this one thing that no one else does. One guy who has seen the other side and then comes back and sticks around for over a month. In that time, he holds firm on eternity and its reality. On his own importance, he is unwavering. And he stands by his reoccurring decision to view and treat the soul as eternal and the body as temporal and replaceable. If that is true, then when maladies strike, we must trust him, his vision, his experience, his word.

It is logical that we don't. I look down and see my legs. Right now, I do. If they suddenly stop working, my first prayer is not for a peace that surpasses understanding but for freakin' legs that work. "Hey, fix these! Amen!"

But Jesus claims to see beyond. He's been there. He's from there. I will have my legs a few more decades. Then I'll die and have new legs. Maybe less scrawny ones? What dreams may come, right? But my soul ... well, I just have the one. It's the headliner and ticket to legs and all the rest.

Jesus heals. Jesus saves. He does so with the internal focus, prioritizing the line of eternity over the blip of this present moment. When he adds a physical component to this, it isn't greater. The great thing is the cheeseburger. The physical is the mint they throw in at the bottom of the bag. When they leave the mint out, I don't go back, complain, and despair. No, I have the cheeseburger. The cheeseburger is the crescendo.

And in this story the cheeseburger is that this paralytic man is forgiven by the God of the universe through no work of his own. It is unmerited, unearned grace, mercy, and love that touches beyond a worldly leap—it disrupts the fabric of eternity.

In this lovely passage, Jesus sees these friends. Can you see them up there on that rooftop? At that moment when their friend is healed and stands up? I bet they go nuts. A party going on above, much like the heavenly celebration when any of us is touched by the healing grace of Jesus. Jesus sees them. He sees the ex-paralytic man. He sees the crowd there witnessing this. He sees the scribes.

And he meets all at the measure of their faith. The crowd came for a show, and a show is what they get. The friends seek an unmistakable blessing, and celebrate an unmistakable blessing. The man desires a new beginning—I wonder how many times, alone at night, he has prayed for a single step. Spiritually and physically, he gets to walk it out.

He sees them all. And he sees us.

The party must have raged that day. If that were my friend, we'd be kicking the soccer ball or playing Twister or leg-wrestling. Anything. Everything. *Let's Peloton!*

Do you think the ex-paralytic slept that night? I think "The Electric Slide" was on repeat in his home. He was testing those babies out.

And the faithless scribes? They missed it. The party was raging, and they missed it. They entered with skeptical resentment, and it is murderously redoubled—Hell grows by consuming itself. Their cynicism and bias kept their own legs from dancing, souls from healing. They, in truth, are the paralyzed ones.

I visited Oxford once. I camouflaged myself in a cardigan and snuck into the town in case they had some sort of IQ forcefield up. The school was cool. Too many books for my liking. No football team. Wasn't exactly Arizona State, okay? While the academia was nice, what I was really after was a pub. *The* pub. The one where The Inklings met—where J.R.R. Tolkien, C.S. Lewis, and their friends would meet to discuss life.

Trouble is, Oxford takes itself super seriously. No kitsch allowed. I expected the outside of the pub to look like a cheap used car lot. Big signs and maybe some of those guys who flail about in the wind. But nope—the town is collectively unassuming in its learned refinement. Wordsworthian, I wandered lonely as a cloud. But hungrier than one. Finally, after hours of searching, I settled on the next pub I came to. I ordered a ham and pineapple and took a stool at a corner table. There was a fire. I leaned back and hit my head on a placard behind me. I turned to see a black and white photo with a caption that said something like, "Here sat J.R.R. Tolkien, C.S. Lewis, and …"

I was sat in the very seat of my desire! By accident. I laughed, took a drink, stared at an adjacent fire, and was hit with a deep loneliness. How much better would this be with a friend? We might have found it sooner, too. What if that friend had known a better way to get where I needed to be? A fireside conversation—party of one—leaves quite a bit on the table. No, this would have been better with a friend.

And so it is in life.

Together we can find Jesus and sit by the fires of his warmth and fellowship. Faith is hard. The trenches of life are deep. We ought not go at it alone.

3. FAMILY

One of the best parts about living abroad was coming home. Europe was great, but distance makes the heart grow fonder, so, as a young man finishing college, I journeyed home for the holidays. One of those first nights back at our family home, I ventured out, likely to buy Christmas presents at the last minute. I returned to a house aglow, a scene of Rockwellian splendor; I gazed on amid the gently falling snow. While I was away, my sisters had arrived from out-of-town with their significant others. Many of our friends, and the friends of our parents, had also joined for a visit, each window depicting a beautiful warmth: here, my mother lovingly laying out a spread on the dining room table; there, people laughing and preparing a group game. It was a picture of family.

Or, at least, one picture. The Bible presents another one.

"Though my father and mother forsake me ..." begins Psalm 27:10. What? Forsake me? Does that actually happen? Like, bad parenting? Neglect? Abuse? Dismissal and abandonment? Unfortunately, we don't need sarcasm font for my line of naive questioning. We all have seen familial wreckage; many of us have lived it.

Or how about Mark 10:29—"'Truly I tell you,' Jesus replied, 'no one who has left home or brothers or sisters or mother or father or children or field for me and the gospel ...'" Wait ... so the gospel can actually divide families—is that what Jesus is saying? That we have some Bible-based abandonment going on?

In Mark 3:31-33, Jesus doesn't just talk about it, he seems to live it: "Then Jesus' mother and brothers arrived. Standing outside, they sent someone in to call him. A crowd was sitting around him, and they told him, 'Your mother and brothers are outside looking for you.'

'Who are my mother and brothers?' Jesus asked."

Yikes. That is like calling someone you can see, witnessing her check her phone, click ignore, and move along, totally neglecting you. Add to this that Jesus' culture was extremely patriarchal. Family was everything. And Jesus publicly shrugs off a societal lynchpin.

These stormy scriptural scenes might sound a bit more accurate than the snowy holiday one I painted. Family is challenging. It can cause deep, terrible wounds. Within the construct is abuse and turmoil and tension. Even good family can wield an unsettling result. My wife was extremely close to her excellent mother. Then that mother died unexpectedly. Now each Mother's Day is like a wake, a wave of overwhelming sadness and longing. Even when we win at family, there seems to be searing loss smuggled in.

Is that why Jesus is disavowing his family in Mark's scene? Is he railing against its temporal nature? Is he really disavowing his family or is this some kind of prank or something? What is going on here?

To understand the climax, we have to flashback to the build-up. The tale begins with Jesus entering a non-snowy house party. He's there and so is much of the town. Again. If you recall Mark 2, Jesus was at a house, and so was much of the town. At that throwdown, the roof, the roof, the roof was not on fire, but it came off all the same. Yes, they blew the roof off the place, and a lame man was lowered down—call him the first ceiling fan if you'd like. Then that lame man was healed and walked out of the joint. There ain't no party like a Jesus party. Can you imagine the neighbors—*those* neighbors. The joyless, nosy ones we all have. They were across the street with a pair of binoculars.

"They're gathering again," the husband mutters disapprovingly to his wife.

"Are the mules everywhere?"

"Yep, everywhere. All parked facing the wrong direction too."

"Is that paralytic fellow there again? You know, the one who can walk."

"Yep, I see him. He's breakdancing."

"Well, Todd, we can't just sit here and watch the neighborhood burn down. We have to do something."

"I know, Margo!"

They do something—or someone does. The authorities are called. But first, Jesus' family is alerted. They come on over to the house party saying, "Jesus is out of his mind."

I love this. First, this is a common reaction. Really, it should be. This is their Jesus—they've seen him grow up, scrape knees; they were there when his voice changed, when it went from angelic to frog-like seemingly overnight. Oh, the joys of puberty. They saw that. They've seen all of it. So when this man, this family member of theirs, claims to be God, they know better. And they are right … *unless*. *Until*. Because if Jesus is God, everything changes—it has to. Every time this happens—that someone claims deity—they are wrong. But what if this was the one time it was true? Well, if that were the case, reality inverts: night becomes day; as the supernatural is unleashed, everything changes.

You see, unbelief is sensible because it is safe. Unbelief—a world in which there is no supernatural realm—is, therefore, natural. We can work hard, save our money, retire. Everything is predictable and I can pretend like I have some modicum of control over my lot and my life. That is the beauty of skepticism—it is safe. Calling Shakespeare the greatest playwright of all time was risky; calling him an "upstart crow" was not.[24] Unless, of course, he Hamlets his way into the hearts of humanity. Unless, of course, you are wrong. Unbelief is safe if it is true. If it is not true—then it is a daily dance with destruction. With belief, unbelief is dismissed and so are limitations. In the realm of belief, blind people see, the paralyzed dance, and death loses its sting. All things become possible. It is a wild-wild westward-leading-still-proceeding existence where hope and truth and justice run madly in all directions.[25] Jesus' family doesn't believe because it feels so much safer. The odds are ever in their favor with that bet. But what if this one time, the longshot pays?

The second thing I love about the family is that they love Jesus. They come after him. Isn't that beautiful? They don't call the cops. They don't roll their eyes and write him out of the will. They don't banish him from the holidays. No, they come after him. And since they don't believe he is God, they default to a mental health condition. Do you catch what this means? It means Jesus isn't a punk! It means they love him because he is so very loveable. A lot of people claim lordship because they are terrible. They want to manipulate people, start a cult, make a bunch of money, prey on the simple, start a war. Not *their* Jesus. *He would never. He must be sick. Jesus, do you have a fever? Are you feeling like yourself?* They diagnose his mind because they've seen his heart. At the personal level, the people who knew Jesus best may not have trusted his divine nature, but they stood firm in his character, his kindness, and his integrity.

While all this is going on, those neighbors must have escalated things. Someone did. Because the authorities show up. The teachers of the law strut up because that is what they do—they strut. People who strut always judge everyone who doesn't strut. When you see someone strutting around, just know they are judging around too; it is part of the deal.

The family strides up and thinks Jesus is sick; the authorities strut up and think Jesus is the Devil. The family knows his goodness so ascribes a mental illness; the religious leaders can see only the worst possible explanation. It is funny how the people with the hardest hearts always seem to have the strongest opinions about the hearts of everyone else. The positions of these two groups present two of the three most common historical positions on Jesus: lunatic and liar.[26] A guy who wanders around for three years claiming to be God and to have the ability to grant eternity to folks? Well, that can't just be a regular dude. *That's Uncle Jesus—isn't he eccentric!* No, he's cray. That or he's a tyrant. With everyone on the edge of their seats, trying to sort out which it is, Jesus sets them straight by sharing a parable that doesn't make any sense.

He starts out all right, appealing to the logic of his critics: "How can Satan drive out Satan?"[27] Okay, not bad. Yeah, if he were Satan, why would he be attacking himself? Doesn't add up. This feels a little like the pageant contestant who gets asked about world peace and says something like, "We just need more love …" but then instead of stopping, she yammers on about Area 51 and puppies and why we'd all be better off if we could eat rainbows. Jesus could have won the crowd by keeping it simple. But here's the thing: Jesus isn't interested in winning the crowd. He is interested in winning the lost. He is speaking for the ages, and he is all about truth, not protection or popularity. So, with that in mind, he blows through the stop lights, sharing a parable about a Kingdom with a prince and a house or castle with a strong man:

If a kingdom is divided against itself, that kingdom cannot stand. If a house is divided against itself, that house cannot stand. And if Satan opposes himself and is divided, he cannot stand; his end has come. In fact, no one can enter a strong man's house without first tying him up. Then he can plunder the strong man's house. Truly I tell you, people can be forgiven all their sins and every slander they utter, but whoever blasphemes against the Holy Spirit will never be forgiven; they are guilty of an eternal sin.[28]

Huh? Well, okay. Maybe his family is right? I mean, that last part sounds like a line straight from Meatloaf … "I would do anything for love, but I won't do that!"[29] What is Jesus talking about? This is like having a perfectly good casserole and finding some rubber bands and marshmallows thrown in for funsies. How does all this tie together?

The answer: Family. Family ties this passage together.

To catch it, we go back to the first family. God made everything in categories, and the sixth category—the ultimate one—was humans. A man and a woman. A family. And this first family sins, causing a separation from God and an eviction from their paradisical home. Yet notice that they are expelled *together*. Adam and Eve. Eve and Adam. God keeps the family intact. Family remained. Yet family was flawed. We see the brokenness in subtle oppression and dominance. Less subtle, we see it in their offspring as one son murders the other. The impetus of this fall is Satan—the thief who comes to steal, kill, and destroy.[30] A pattern emerges: over and over and over God works through family. Over and over and over Satan seeks to destroy family.

Take the story of Noah. God saves humanity through a family. To quote Modest Mouse, "They all float on, okay."[31] But then they hit dry land and it is not okay. Noah gets drunk and naked, a state no son revels in finding his father.[32] Yuck. A curse follows, making it clear: Here we find an echo of Adam and Eve and the narrative of Eden—nakedness, shame, and curse.

Or how about Abraham, who is told that his descendants would be a great nation that would outnumber the stars. That promise hinges on family. God is again working through family, offering a familial blessing to fulfill a familial promise. Abraham and Sarah eventually realize this blessing in Isaac, but first they make a big mess of things through objectifying a servant and attempting to operate outside of God's provision—again, an echo of Eden.

This is the tension that recurs throughout scripture. Families are enslaved and enslavers. Families are misguided. Families are ravaged. And yet, families are chosen by God—accepted, forgiven, safeguarded: "I will be your God and you will be my *people*."

This cosmic tug-of-war between destruction and redemption ensues, and something has to give.

Remember Harry Potter? He was this boy wizard. Had a notable scar. In the first Harry Potter book, this evil character tries to kill Harry, but the body he is using cannot touch Harry; any contact made with Harry causes severe burns.[33] Later Dumbledore tells Harry why he couldn't be touched: "It was because of your mother. She sacrificed herself for you, and that kind of act leaves a mark."[34]

The Bible says something similar in 1 John 5:18: "We know that everyone who has been born of God does not keep sinning, but he who was born of God protects him, and the evil one does not touch him."

Something has to give. Or *someone*.

Snap back to reality, back to the *Gospel of Mark* …

The prince/strongman in the parables Jesus shares is Satan. The thief who comes to steal, to kill, and to destroy. He snatched family from God. He pulls the rope taut: father wounds, mommy issues, abuse, oppression, hatred. Steal. Kill. Destroy.

But then a king/strongerman shows up. Not only does this hero pull the rope, but he uses it to bind the prince/strongman. This hero plunders the house, taking back and safeguarding family from the clutch of the evil one: "The evil one does not touch him." Because of the One, we cannot be touched. The age-old tension is resolved.

That is why we can complete the passages with which we began this chapter (with the blissful resolution in bold):

Though my father and mother forsake me, **the Lord will receive me** *(Psalm 27:10).*

"Truly I tell you," Jesus replied, "no one who has left home or brothers or sisters or mother or father or children or fields for me and the gospel will fail to receive **a hundred times as much in this present age: homes, brothers, sisters, mothers, children** *and fields—along with persecutions—and in the age to come eternal life (Mark 10:29-30).*

"Who are my mother and my brothers?" he asked. Then he looked at those seated in a circle around him and said, "Here are my mother and my brothers! **Whoever does God's will is my brother and sister and mother"** *(Mark 3:33-35).*

I always had modest expectations for my marriage. I thought, reasonably, that I would live in the kind of household wherein my wife would be waiting for me when I got home from work. She'd be delighted to see me; she'd be scantily clad (obviously!) and have something wonderful for me to eat, as she listened to my every word and rubbed my shoulders. Totally simple, reasonable, fair-minded expectations, right?

Instead, early in marriage, coming home was like playing the game Marco Polo with a quiet kid. I'd get home and finally find my wife, and she'd look at me with a face that said, *Oh, it's you again.*

"I live here!" I'd remind her.

And then this one day came. I opened the garage, and there she was. *It's happening!* I thought. It only took five years, but finally, she loves me—*she really loves me.* I got out of the car, and she started crying … and then I saw her hand. In it was a pregnancy test. After three difficult years navigating infertility, she got to announce, through tears, "We are having a baby!"

She could have just as easily and truthfully said, "We are adding to our family!" And that is what Jesus is saying here.

Something had to give. Or someone …

Jesus. He gave his life. He spilled his blood. If I'm researching my lineage, determining my family, I'll look to the blood. With Jesus, we look to the bloodshed. That by that blood, we've been adopted, safeguarded, invited. That we can sing that goofy "Father Abraham" Sunday school song. That we can say, with utter confidence, "My dad can beat up your dad!" Accepted, valued, loved. A new family has been created—the church is the family.

If I choose it. If I choose a third category from the aforementioned trilemma. That Jesus is not a lunatic, nor is he a liar. "Whoever does God's will …" verse 35 claims. *Whoever* chooses Jesus as Lord is welcomed into the family forever.

Which brings us back to the Meatloaf-lyric verse that says all these things will be forgiven, except that one thing. In part, that one thing is not choosing the family of God. It is denying the wooing of God's Spirit. There is an invite to belong and we either claim full inheritance, or it is a full denial. We get all the blessings of family or none of them. And, on this earth, perhaps the greatest blessing we get to partake in is the joy that comes in loving one another. That we come together, as a church, to tell stories about Dad. Jesus says the way we recognize his family—the family crest, if you will—is how we love one another. The church should be a vision of a redefined, redeemed, rediscovered family. We have this picture of family in the origin story of Eden. We have a familial sense in the heavenly gathering around the throne of God. In the beginning and the end, we witness sacred community, togetherness. And in the middle? It is family that serves as the bridge, built on the adoption by God made possible through his Strongerman son. It is a love-deep adoption whose papers are signed in blood.

I recall standing in the snow and looking up at the family home that night all those years ago. It was a picturesque scene: the laughter, an echoing joy; the fare, deeper nourishment for the soul; the fire and light, a warmth eternal.

Now imagine the host is Jesus, opening wide the door, smile wider, saying, "Come in, brother" or "Come in, sister." Truly, a homecoming like no other.

Here are my mother and brothers and sisters ...

Will we enter? Will we join and become that family?

4. EVIL

I'll routinely watch through *The Office* and I always get choked up at the end of the series. Good shows, good stories, do this to us—they make us feel like we are part of the show, that these are, in some way, our stories. This power is in storytelling, but the thrust of that storytelling is the power of moments. Iconic shows have iconic moments. For *The Office* one such moment comes on the Niagara Falls ship the *Maid of the Mist*, where Jim and Pam, the main romantic thread that runs through the show, have set foot to elope. They have fled their wedding and its awkward formality (and more awkward friends), and there with the waterfalls raging in the background, their future sails forward on the smooth waters of loving commitment.

But it wasn't actually supposed to be this way—this iconic moment. All the way through the table read, the script painted a much different scene. In that version, Dwight—the show's misfit punchline—has commandeered a horse. He rides to the edge of the falls, and then on some wild impulse, he and the horse plunge over the falls.[35]

Steve Carell called the bit a "cartoon joke," and reasoned with the showrunner that it would be unwise and unfunny to kill a horse on network television. It all seemed far-fetched for a show that strode, in its early years, to stay somewhat true to life. The death of a horse was anything but.

Discretion is the better part of valor, and no horses were harmed, nor appeared, in this episode. Instead, we just have the splendor of the falls, the beauty of love, and an iconic TV moment.

You can't help but think, in reading Mark 5, that Mark needed Steve Carell. In the questionable version presented, we get the longest exorcism in the Bible.[36] I once wrote a guide through the *Gospel of Mark*, and a leader who was supporting the project asked me, "Next time can you pick something other than Mark?" His reason was simple: the pigs. A bunch of demon-filled pigs hurtle over a cliffside to their deaths. Paul famously says, "For I am not ashamed of the gospel …" *Yes, Paul, I'm with you. Go gospel! Good news! Team Jesus all the way!* However, I am a smidge ashamed of the pigs.

It is a section one wishes could be sliced from scripture. It joins the great Jonah-gobbling fish, the parting of seas, walking on water, and the virgin birth. Demon-possession? Here we go again! It's modernity—you'd think we could do better. That we could trim superstition, trust science, and be a bit more self-respecting in our religious ideals.

Brings to mind Matthew 11:16-19. In that passage, Jesus applies a musical analogy to non-believers—that no matter what the prophets or Jesus did, the opposite would be demanded as the requirement for belief. To lend his idea a more modern idiom: "Damned if you do, damned if you don't."

For many of us, we come to the Bible with an eyeroll and mutter, "Can we just cut the miracles?" It would be so much easier to explain our beliefs, to stand firm in those beliefs, without all the magic hoopla. Of course, if we did, indeed, cut the miracles, what is left? What would be different about Jesus? What would distinguish him from other biographies, on Diogenes or Plato, Churchill or Roosevelt? If the Bible were stripped of the supernatural, it would not—*surprise!*—be supernatural any longer. There are plenty of natural stories that are lovely and true. What the Bible claims, even in its strangeness, is to be something different: lovelier and truer even. With a common book, sans miracles, we would shout for the supernatural—*do something, God! Show me! Prove it!* This was the claim of the Old Testament skeptics: "Show me your God!"[37]

And Mark answers, "Okay." And as soon as he does, marching some pigs off a cliff, we revert back to cynicism: *Nice fairy tales. Enjoy your Flying Spaghetti Monster.*

That can't happen, we say.

And we are right! That's the point!

The Bible is weird—full stop. It is supposed to be! It claims not to be from this world, rather to be God-breathed, an echo of how the world should be, an overture of how it will be. So, we come to Mark 5 and should be unsurprised that Mark drops us in the deep end.

It begins lakeside, as so many things do. (Shameless admission: I fell in love with my to-be wife lakeside. And now, in this book about Jesus, I'm hiding this Easter egg for the sake of romance and to be able to gauge whether or not she read to this point or not. Digression over.) Jesus gets out of a boat and a man approaches with an "impure spirt." *Here we go … Welp, can't give this book to a friend now … here comes the weird ….*

Maybe a good place to start is upriver from the falls. Let's forget the impure spirit/demon possession thing for a moment, and ask instead *Is evil real?*

Most would answer *yes*, even if their mouth says "no." What I mean is best captured in illustrative terms. Imagine you are in a crowd before me, and I have a baseball bat. I then proceed to hit little foam balls as you and the crowd throw them at me. I have a good swing; we are having fun; maybe there are prizes or something? Afterwards, we'd likely agree that it was an altogether good thing happening, and certainly a good and proper use of a baseball bat.

Now, think about the person in all the world you love the most. A child, a spouse, a dear friend, a grandparent. Picture that person's smiling face, tender lines like rivers of goodness. Picture your beloved standing with me, the crowd before us. And now, picture me taking my baseball bat and bludgeoning them.

It is a graphic scene, I know. I'm sorry for it. But should that scene become some morbid reality, not one of you would just sit there and watch contentedly. No, you'd yell, "STOP!" You'd storm the stage. You'd call the authorities. You'd take some mitigating action against me and my assault. Why?

Well, because you'd deem my actions to be misguided. To be misplaced. To be bad. To be wrong. To be … evil.

We occupy a time where moral relativism rules the day. You may not agree, for instance, and rather than saying I'm wrong, you'd say something like, "Well, that's your truth." Your truth—my truth. Everyone has a right to their own truth. Yet for all of our verbal accommodations, we live in one of the most judgmental societies ever, seeking to silence and cancel and condemn. Don't believe me? Read Twitter for, like, eight seconds. You'll find someone getting called out for some moral indiscretion, and this from a society that claims there is no right or wrong.

The stakes are high, for truth is what hangs in the balance. This is why we are so judgmental and so sensitive—good and evil are real as ever, yet we've shifted the standard for such and it is disorienting. *Oughtness* hangs in the balance—who will determine truth?

Despite our fickleness, we tend to agree that evil is real in the way we act. Watch footage from the latest school shooting if you still don't believe me. What you see is tragic. It is sick. It causes pain. I recall Columbine, the first such incident like this I had witnessed. I remember lamenting, naively, that *This will probably happen every four or five years now.* This happens every four or five days, and that is a generous estimate. There is something evil at work when children are massacred.

When we consider evil and its reality, we tend to categorize it into mental, emotional, and physical. These are tidy categories and serve us well as a society focused on the material world. These are diagnostic distinctions that can be triaged and treated—take a pill, listen to a talk, modify behavior through different counseling regimens. Truly, this is helpful.

One area that has been deemed unhelpful is the spiritual classification. Sections like Mark 5 foist upon the world stone age superstitions that claim everything is a demon. The simplistic view of the Bible is truly impractical.

Except that this isn't what the Bible says about evil.

Take Matthew 4:24 as a worthy example. In the scene, people bring to Jesus their sick. These are the ill folks who are being impacted by evil, whether in a participatory sense or in a passive sense in which evil is happening to them. But the text doesn't Oprah things—"You get a demon! And you get a demon! And you get a demon!" No, it lists out the following: "Those suffering with various diseases, those suffering severe pain, the demon-possessed, those having seizures, the paralyzed." Demon-possession is one type of malady among many, meaning the Bible would answer the question *Is evil a result of emotional, mental, physical, or spiritual factors?* with a hardy "Yes."

Yes, evil is emotional. Yes, evil is physical. Yes, evil is mental. Yes, evil is spiritual. Evil is nuanced and interlocking. Evil is complex. The cause and fuel for evil can have a spiritual component. When we revisit the school shooters, do we find emotional damage? What about cognitive disorders and illness? Physically are there often issues? The answer is yes to all of those questions. But is it that far-fetched to claim there may be a spiritual dimension when the answer to someone's problems is the murder of schoolchildren? Perhaps there is another plane at play that our generational snobbery[38] has blinded us to? We are prone to reduce planes, claiming intelligence, yet seldom is a reduction of planes more complex. We reduce it to simplify, if we are honest, and because we like the illusion of control— even though that very decision yields us less and less actual control. The claim that eradication of the spiritual component for evil in our world is a more intelligent prospect is like going from color television to black-and-white because the hues hurt our eyes, yet claiming it is for reasons of sophistication. We cannot run from the idea of evil because it challenges our sensibilities. In doing so, we fail to fully challenge the evil that is ensnaring us.

This highlights for us one of the first realities of evil: evil is complex. The Bible presents this reality time and time again. We believe in evil. We believe we know more and better, enough to dismiss demons. Yet why in our learning and sophistication are we just as evil? We understand mental health better than any civilization; however, our mental health seems to be in a continual state of decline.

When it comes to the demonic, it is easy to play the evidence card—we believe what we can see, after all. But that is like walking out to a wet lawn and finding no evidence for rain. Evil *is* the evidence.

If demons are real, I would contend they are less like monsters under the bed and more like secret agents of evil. They are producing, propagating, and propelling evil thoughts into evil behaviors into evil agendas. In *The Screwtape Letters*, C.S. Lewis tries his hand at demonic workflow in having an elder demon named Screwtape write letters of advice to his young nephew.[39] At the heart of their demonic strategy, according to Lewis, is to allow humans to disbelieve in demons. Non-existence is the best cover for covert destruction. However, if humans do begin to turn a corner on the possibility of demonic existence, Screwtape advises his nephew to make the humans think of demons as caricatures—little red devils, more a joke than anything. Type *devil Halloween costumes* into your web browser and you will find, in popular demand, the precise sort of thing Screwtape had in mind.

We've mentioned John 10:10. In it, Jesus doesn't joke about Satan, the chief demon, saying in seriousness: "He comes to steal, to kill, and to destroy." Steal. Kill. Destroy. Makes sense that perhaps the best way to steal, to kill, and to destroy is to prey on mental illness or to weaponize physical weakness. Recently, I had a friend undergo a dark trial. It was a physical setback, and we discussed how she was doing. During our conversation, she revealed that she was angry at God. What was a physical challenge had become spiritual in nature—the weapon of pain had evolved and gained internal and relational destructive capabilities.

The Bible depicts an adversary, a source for and of decay. We see sickness, pain, wrath, and violence in the Bible; we see sickness, pain, wrath, and violence in our world. It would seem that we are the ones being unknowingly bludgeoned by the enemy's bat.

Along with being complex, evil is progressive. Look at what is says in Mark 5:3-5:

This man lived in the tombs, and no one could bind him anymore, not even with a chain. For he had often been chained hand and foot, but he tore the chains apart and broke the irons on his feet. No one was strong enough to subdue him. Night and day among the tombs and in the hills he would cry out and cut himself with stones.

Verse 3 uses the word *anymore*. The obvious indication, then, is that at some point, he could be bound. Verse 4 offers us a similar structure, claiming that *no one* could subdue him. The only way to make such a claim is if *someone* had subdued him, or at least had tried. Finally, verse 5 says that the man would cut himself with stones. A person can cut himself only so much—at some point the cut will go too far or too deep.

What this speaks to is the trajectory of evil in this instance. This man went from "normal" to odd or eccentric. At some point anger entered the picture. Notice, too, the strength of the man—it is increasing. His physical strength is growing, and this is what evil does. It promises us a strength, but only at a cost. Work to gain that millionaire status, leaving a trail of bodies in your wake, but the cost will be your friends, your health, and, perhaps, your family. Evil gives a faux freedom, a leash that leads to a strangling slavery. Evil progresses. Deeper cuts, deeper isolation, deeper depravity. The trajectory is easy to see for this character (and for us): death.

I'm writing this in an office space right now. It is well-lit and comfortable. So, when I read about this man out in the tombs, howling and bleeding, I am thankful that I am not possessed by a demon. I'm relieved that none of this has any bearing on my life, whatsoever. Sip a cool drink and move on, beyond the reach of evil.

Linguistics, however, challenge this relief. In the Greek, our English "demon-possessed" is closer to *demonized*.[40] So, I may not be demon-possessed—my head isn't spinning around or anything—but could I be demonized in any areas?

Well, a way to test this is to assess my own trajectory—where am I headed in different areas of life? To do this, let's pretend for a moment that I am required to look at illicit images on my phone for at least one minute a day for 30 days. If then, at the end of 30 days, we could evaluate what I chose to look at, how would the early days compare to the end of the month? Would the images I selected be more or less intense? More or less depraved? More or less explicit?

Though the answer would be obvious, the situation is not—it is far-fetched. No one is going to come along and make me do that. But how about if I engage in about 40 hours of career worship a week. For about 40 years. I wonder if I am going to be more or less ensnared by vocational trappings? More or less driven by money? Power? External validation?

Being demonized is not a frothing horror scene. There is no vomit, but it is just as sick. It is subtle, as we are undone by common counterfeits. I become complicit in progressing conditions that are destroying me. It is like erosion—vacationing to a beach and noticing very little change year-over-year. After a decade, though, the beach is half as big as it once was. In two decades, it is washed away entirely, part of an all-consuming sea, which gobbles the sand with an unceasing rhythmic hum.

To paraphrase biblical philosophy: Anything more important than the Lord is your lord. So the question then: What trajectory is your *lord* taking you on? The road to alcoholism begins with a single sip. For our souls, many of us are unknowingly sipping on what we'll eventually drown in. Even seemingly good things like earthly success can just be slavery in smart dress, a well-dressed demon of destruction.

This is where some biblical imagery for the demonic is helpful. In 1 Peter 5, the Devil is pictured as a roaring lion looking for someone to devour. The thing about a hungry lion is that a meal sates its appetite, but then makes it hungrier, for it is now a bigger lion. Which means evil always wants more of you. It never says, "Okay, we've done enough harm. Let's lay off his marriage." No, it will devour to the bone.

Song of Solomon speaks of a symbolic love relationship and warns the young lovers in the tale to catch the little foxes in the vineyards.[41] It is important to catch the little foxes because little foxes become … you got it: big foxes. And big foxes multiply creating more little foxes. You've seen what pets can do. Now imagine a houseful of undomesticated animals. Now realize this: you are the house. The foxes seek to destroy *everything*.

The man in Mark 5 ends up in the tombs. Does our trajectory point there, too, or to life?

Evil is complex. Evil is progressive. And evil is systematized.

In stories like these, it is easy to miss ourselves. You have a really sketchy dude who lives in the cemetery—*nope, not me!*—and you have a guy who

walks on water for kicks. But you also have others in the tale. Here is what
they do: first, they send him to the tombs. They *other* him. We could name
about a million instances of this happening to the person deemed different.
Half of that number happened to me in middle school. The second thing
the villagers do is witness the man's healing, and then? Do they follow
Jesus? Do they throw an exorcism party? Inspired by this story, I still think
it would be fun to go to my local bakery and have the cake decorator make
me a good, old-fashioned exorcism cake. I'd love to see that reaction.

They don't get a cake, though. No exorcism song. Instead, their reaction
is to kindly ask Jesus to leave. Why? Didn't this guy just do a really good
thing for their community and for this neighbor? Why ask him to leave?

Well, first, it goes back to our contention with this story even being *in the
Bible*. We think it is too weird to read about—imagine it happening *in your
life. No, thank you—I'll take what I know*. Truth is, most of us have become
numbly complacent. I've allied with loss and death and pain for long
enough that at least I *know* them. Jesus strolls up by the lake and threatens
the known, the expected; the rote is challenged by a new route. Jesus breaks
the chains, and there is nothing so scary as freedom.

Think of the Israelites. Freed from the shackles of slavery, it took them
about five minutes in the wilderness to pine for Egypt—*at least we knew
when breakfast was or where we were going to sleep!*[42] It is like we have a
Satanic Stockholm Syndrome—we've become attached to our kidnapper
because at least he's ours. And Jesus kicks in the door to the hovel and says,
"No, I have better for you. We're leaving!"

Second, the townsfolk want him to leave because of the pigs. Now, before
we even get to the motivation, let's apply some reason. Some people don't
believe the Bible is anything but fiction—that it is a bunch of made-up
tales doctored and used to control the masses or something. Passages like
this make that a hard position to take. What writer ever would, when

trying to make a story plausible, think, *You know, let's throw in some demon possession, with a side of bacon.* It isn't like this is some common trope or stolen from tales passed about from other cultures: "Grandpa, Grandpa, tell the one about the great swine slaughter!" If the Bible were some coercive, corroborated effort, this episode never would have made it in. And what sort of weirdo just makes this up? Demon possession and deliverance? Sure, I can get there—it seems like a sensible contrivance. But Mark had to be some sort of nutjob to interject these pigs from imagination. Perhaps someone said they'd believe in Jesus "when pigs fly" and he put this in as a rhetorical wink-wink? I think the most logical response to this story is that—whatever happened before it—a bunch of little piggies went wee-wee-wee all the way (and eternally) home.

And this biblical bay of pigs is what disinvites Jesus from the area, thanks to a culturally acceptable evil, then and now—the love of money. These pigs represent the livelihood of a person, or, more likely, a group of investors. Someone owns the pigs and pays others to tend to the pigs. We see an economic structure going down the drain.

I work in a secular institution that allows for faith exploration. When we started a Faith & Community department, some of our executives visited a company that had faith as part of the workplace. On this visit, our leaders spent time with that company's legal team and asked how they avoid or limit litigation. The answer was a bit surprising. After talking about being wise and loving toward people, and eliminating coercion and some other practical advice, the lawyer in charge said, "But at the end of the day, you have to ask, 'What is the price of a soul?'"

This is the question that is asked to the villagers in this scene. *What is the price of a soul?* Their demon-possessed neighbor is restored, his trajectory augmented, his future and hope renewed, and they look on and ask if there is a BOGO sale. Any cheaper souls around? Maybe a Groupon or something? Simply put, this man, to them, was not worth the price of

2,000 pigs. And really, it wasn't even about these pigs, was it? They were lost. Gone. Truly a sunk cost. Jesus is asked to leave for the fear of what he might do next. Today it is the pigs, but what of tomorrow? *Our fields, our companies, our precious savings!* Eternity? Healing? Renewal? Victory over evil? *Um, we'll take the cash, please.* Property. Control. They'd willingly save their bacon over their souls.

The townsfolk were blinded by a system, so they couldn't recognize or accept a pattern of change. Economics. Materialism. Capitalism. There are systems all around us. Most aren't sinister in nature. They aren't even bad in nature. They are neutral things that become monstrous when they become main things. It can be youth sports and how we structure our family around them. It can be the way we forever foist our better days to some ethereal retirement. It can be the way our culture somehow now makes one feel compelled to watch about 83 shows a month. In the 1980s, a study found that Americans would spend something like 15 years of their lives watching TV![43] Television isn't wrong, but when it becomes a systemized way to rob you of life, it sounds an awful lot like theft: Steal. Kill. Destroy.

This systemization is happening to all of us. Think about political radicalization. Many people reading these words right now do not realize that they've been radicalized by politics. If I say something like, "I think the president is doing a really great job," about half of you would slam this book shut (and shut me out of your life) in a huff. This is a problem, but the worst part about it? You don't even know it is happening to you—that it has happened to you. Others do. This is why your presence at Thanksgiving is making your loved ones sweat, if you are even still being invited.

Systemized evil is luring all of us all of our lives. W.H. Auden felt this firsthand when he went to a movie in New York. In that film house were good people—intellectuals, poets, cultural elites. Smart and wise. The film featured Hitler's invasion of Poland, and when Jews were shown on screen, these smart and wise people yelled slurs. "Kill them!" they jeered.[44]

Auden was aghast. How could this be the position of the "good" people? We could ask the same for so many millions who have held slaves, hurled hatred, cursed their fellow human. For Auden, this revealed to him something about evil—that it doesn't have red horns and a spiky tail. That most humans don't set out to be villains. That the world is not neatly made up of categories: good and bad people. No, this incident came with a behind-the-scenes look at the soft, sinister footsteps of evil and it caused a shudder in him. For he knew, too, that though it preyed on him in other ways, being devoured is being devoured.

This glimpse of evil actually led Auden toward a faith in God. This seems counter-intuitive, but indeed a major impetus for belief in God is the presence of evil.[45] We want an answer to that great question, a hero to win the day, good to prevail. And if evil is complex and progressive and systematized, we need a God who is complex and progressive and systematically good and powerful. We see a glimpse of that, too, in Jesus as the scene plays out.

In this passage, evil is confronted. Jesus doesn't avoid the demonized man. He doesn't shy away. He doesn't see the beggar at the stoplight and get in the farthest possible lane. Nor will God forsake the evil in, on, or around our lives. Physically we suffer with cancer, with fibromyalgia, with back pain. Mentally, we have anxiety, disorders and fear. Emotionally, heartaches harangue us. We are trapped by traumas—there is no English word for trauma's opposite, an unrelenting joy that readily resurfaces.[46] None of these afflictions will escape a graveside confrontation with the living Christ.

Not only is evil confronted—that is fine and well, but what good is a losing confrontation? No, in this passage evil is overpowered. Exorcisms tend to follow a script, regardless of belief-set. "By the power of _____, I compel you." The blank is filled with gods, or witchdoctors, or rulers. Historically, the power is dialed up in this manner. Jesus doesn't play that song and dance. He looks evil in the eye and says directly, "Come out." It is almost like he is bored—"Ugh, give me something hard to do." It reminds me of that scene from *Raiders of the Lost Ark*. Indiana Jones is running around in a crowd when an enemy swordsman approaches. The crowd parts; the audience readies for a classic movie fight scene. The swordsman proceeds to flaunt his skills, flexing pre-fight. Indy sighs, wipes his brow, rolls his eyes, and then pulls out a revolver and shoots his opponent through the heart, before turning and hurrying toward a bigger objective. That is Jesus here. "Ya'll call that power? Let's get on with it. I have a world that needs saving."

It is a callback to the strongman in Mark 3. Jesus tells the parable about the strongman being Satan, and then, here, we get a picture of how that encounter actually plays out. The strongman gets in there and he dominates. Thousands of demons versus one lonely soul, and it is a blowout—the man is isolated, miserable, and harming himself. Then the Strongerman strides up. Jesus turns this into an utter mismatch, transforming the swaggering legion of demons into a whimpering, simpering, sickly gaggle of wretches, unmasked and afraid. The unspoken promise pictured here is clear: the evil in our lives is doomed when we take it to Jesus.

Thank goodness this script made it past the table read. Especially for this last reason: evil is conquered. The suffering man is depicted in verse 15 as "dressed and in his right mind." He is among the people. Moments prior, for who knows how long, this man had been among the tombs, the dead, naked. Crying out. Alone.

Now, in verse 15, he is alive. Crying out all that Jesus had done for him. Restored to life. Clothed. Trajectory: reclaimed and renewed.

Jesus, by these people, was asked to depart. He would, but he wouldn't leave them with their evil. Instead, he'd be stripped naked, blood spilled, crying out, alone. Among the dead. In the tomb.

This is a cautionary-turned-redemption tale of evil infecting from the inside out. But Jesus flips it inside out by doing the same thing to evil itself. He trades places with this man, with us, going to the heart of death itself in love, losing everything and giving everything. Conquering evil once and for all.

And, just as he does for this man, Jesus will make all things new, restored to life. Trajectory: reclaimed and renewed.

5. REST

Good, it's just us. Last chapter, we used the careening pigs to run off the masses, and I think we're alone now. So allow me, dear, loyal reader, to make a loving proclamation: You are doing life wrong.

Still here? Wow, okay. We'll press on then. The reason I claim that you are doing life wrong is because I am doing life wrong. Evil has slinked into our lives and instead of living our lives, we have life just sort of happen to us. Remember that evil is systematized, and these systems snake their way into the gardens of our existence under the guise of normalcy. Ideas and ways of life slither in, eventually working their way round our necks, choking the life from us.

I don't jog, but I recall when I was made to do so on athletic teams. In college, I thought headphones would help the tedious monotony. But on those early morning six-mile runs, I noticed erratic times caused by erratic energy. The root problem was the pace—it was inconsistent. And this inconsistency was due to the music that was blaring through the headphones—my pace followed the tempo of the songs. The fast songs were killing me, disallowing me from properly managing the energy necessary to finish the course well.

This is us. We are being undone by destructive rhythms. We are hypnotically marching nowhere to the thrumming beat, one we haven't chosen.

Or let's take the scenic route to get where I'm driving: The other day I was conversing with a friend, and I told what I thought was a rather good story about two men. My friend chuckled at the punchline of the story, but then added an editorial note: "It would be even better if they had been twins!"

Nothing beats a good joke correction. It is like giving a sermon: pouring your heart, sweat, and tears into a talk, engaging in public speaking, a thing that most people fear just ahead of their fear of death, and then stepping down to a waiting audience member. There is always someone just right there—it is like they apparated into your hula-hoop of space. They usually begin with a backhanded compliment: "Gosh, for someone so inexperienced, you sure talk really fast." You say *thanks* even though it feels like *sorry* would probably fit better. The person then proceeds to bring up a theological perspective that probably doesn't have much to do with the talk you just gave, but they think it is incredibly important that you understand how an obscure verse from a minor prophet is vital to unpack right now, before the second service begins. They'll also add that you use your hands wrong, look a bit shabby, and did a really, really great job for someone who can't read. You tell them you can read, and they just laugh and laugh. Then they'll give you a note they made during the boring parts of your sermon, and close with, "Also, twins. It would have been better if you'd included some twins!"

I didn't like the correction my friend made. But I liked it even less because of how immensely correct she was. Of course it would have been better with twins! Everything is. Twins are fascinating. They are interesting, with their secret languages and shared intuition. Twins are creepy. *The Shining* knew a random ghost-kid would be terrifying, but slap some twins in the mix and we can't ever look at a tricycle the same way. Seriously, that could have been the whole movie—just those twins riding around an abandoned hotel. Ugh!

Twins are captivating. I gave this some thought, and I think I figured out why: Twins look alike. Pretty good for someone inexperienced who may or may not be able to read, right? That's it, though. Twins look alike, and this is compelling to non-twins, this mirrored image.

All this was going through my head after my friend critiqued my joke, and then another thought invaded: *What if Hitler had been a twin?* Can you imagine life for that guy—Hitler's twin? He'd stroll into a Berlin convenience store to grab a brat, and the place would go silent with patrons thinking they were in the presence of the Fuhrer. Many zealots would worship the twin, loving his brother's maniacal machinations. Yet much of the world would loathe the twin on sight. If he struck off on a holiday in the south of France, he wouldn't be coming home.

If you were Hitler's twin, you'd be looking for a razor real quick. Growing out the hair. Wearing some wedges for a little lift. Anything to distance yourself from your immoral, sadistic brother. You'd desire a life that is better, freer.

Now, what if Hitler's twin were non-identical? There would still be some familial resemblance, but in the common sibling fashion. And what if Hitler's non-identical twin recognized the evil way his brother was leading and living? Well, it would be ludicrous, then, to don a little military uniform, grow a caterpillar 'stache, comb the hair over, and start barking at people.

This is a good time to ask: *What are we even talking about here?*

This: That believers in Jesus are supposed to be transformed. Shifted. Different. Pursuing the process of change. Liberated. Enlightened by the very light of Christ. We may carry on a familial resemblance with the world, but we have the choice at our disposal to alter our appearance—to look different, to live different, and to present a different way to others.

Now, let me be clear—I am not saying that all unbelievers are Hitler. But

I am saying that if there is a way, and then there is a better way, we'd be foolish to continue our pursuits on the inferior path. Yet, that is what we do. We continue our constant attempts at twinning with this world and its way. I walk like the world, think like the world; it's mannerisms are my mannerisms. It is a mirror image.

If this is the case, then again, I am doing life wrong. I'm missing out on flourishing. And I'm doing so in a sneaky, acceptable, oft-applauded way. My guess is that you are too.

Mark 6:31-32 are simple verses: "Then, because so many people were coming and going that they did not even have a chance to eat, Jesus said to them, 'Come with me by yourselves to a quiet place and get some rest.' So they went away by themselves in a boat to a solitary place."

At the height of action, in the midst of ministry and miracle, in frenetic comings and goings, Jesus doesn't prescribe moralism. He doesn't demand hard work; he doesn't chide his followers to pull themselves up by their bootstraps. He doesn't motivate them to stand out, nor does he heap religion on them. He doesn't tell them to be the change they want to see in the world or to #disrupt. No, instead he says, "Let's rest."

Rest. Renewal. Peace. These are what Jesus prescribes.

"Let's rest."

Can you hear him say that?

This is not a standalone concept for Jesus. It is at the heart of who he is, what he stands for, and how he lives. In Matthew 11, he says:

Come to me, all you who are weary and burdened, and I will give you rest. Take my yoke upon you and learn from me, for I am gentle and humble in heart, and you will find rest for your souls. For my yoke is easy and my burden is light.

Are you weary? Burdened? Have you run back and forth to 17 practices this week? You've had 22 meetings, need to log 50 miles, must read 75 pages, and all of this—and more—has to be done at 100 MPH. Jesus looks at this—and more—and doesn't give a life hack. He gives himself. His way. Rest. Renewal. Peace.

In the gospels, we see Jesus walking lakeside. Escaping to pray and seeking solitude. My four-year-old has begun, in moments of flustering emotions, to demand his need for "alone time." Jesus gets that. We see a storm rage, and Jesus is asleep. He tells his followers to consider the lilies of the valley; it is because he already has considered them. He notices the fig trees. Lets his hands linger and touch the fields of wheat.

Jesus is a picture of rest, renewal, and peace. Are you?

I imagine you use the world's most acceptable answer when asked how you are doing. That answer is, "Busy." Busy is a badge of honor. *Look at all these plates I have spinning! Look at how bloodshot my eyes are! Look at me sieze the day—or is this me being seized by it? No time to consider: busy, busy, busy!* The second-leading answer on the Family Feud board would be "good," which is just a substitute for the longer truth: "I'm too busy to talk to you right now!"

Can you hear Jesus answering that way? *Lord, heal my young daughter? Jesus, what did that parable mean? Jesus, can we play?* This last one happened. Some kids approached Jesus,[47] which probably says something about how he was—kids actually wanted to be near him. Jesus very easily could have taken a page out of our book, "No, I'm busy. Got a world to save and all." I mean, that is a pretty killer excuse. If I can be too busy for my own kids because of email, I think Jesus had every right to be too busy for stranger-kids due to the demands of being a vocational Messiah.

But Jesus doesn't say, "Busy." His disciples do. They try to protect their leader's sacred time. But Jesus realizes that time is made sacred in how we give it away. He says, "Let the little children come to me."

I realized I was doing life wrong a few years ago. Again, pretty good for a guy with so little experience. Anyway, I had Saturday to myself with my then two-year-old. We had all day, and one thing on the entire agenda: go to the library. In order to go to the library, we had to do seven things—put on a fresh diaper (him, not me), two socks, two shoes, shorts, and a shirt. Each of these things should take seven seconds. Stopwatches at the ready— here we go. Thing is, MJ started kicking and squirming and giggling. I warned him to be still or else, getting louder and louder. My volume only intensified his playfulness—*little fool was going to make us late!* "FINE, NO LIBRARY!" I shouted after three-minutes of trying to get him dressed. A few minutes later, I pulled up the library website—they were open for 12 hours that day. We had 12 hours, yet a 30-second delay sets me off.

Jesus had real issues, a bit beyond a trip to the library. Like in Mark 5, when this big deal guy approached Jesus, a synagogue leader. This man needed help, and he was an influential guy, the type of person we all want to help. The disciples surely saw this as being good for business. And the big deal guy had a big deal situation: his daughter was dying. Stopwatches at the ready—here we go.

As they walked to the man's home, a sick woman in the crowd touched Jesus' garment.

Jesus stops. You can almost hear the groans of the disciples, "Oh no. Here we go. He's at it again."

They try to talk Jesus out of finding the person who touched him—"Uh, big crowd, JC. Maybe we need to focus on the medical emergency at hand, yeah?"

But Jesus was unrelenting. Sensing this, the woman approaches, admitting that it was she who had touched his cloak. Don't miss Jesus' response in verse 34; it is so lovely: "Daughter, your faith has healed you. Go in peace and be freed from your suffering."

Jesus brings the woman rest, renewal, and peace, but he also does something else in that. He loves her. Here was a person who felt unworthy. It was a woman in a society that held women in low regard. Added to that, it was a sick woman. She was so timid, she was willing and worthy only of touching Jesus' garment—truly, a cloak-and-dagger healing. But the dagger came from Jesus, and it was a piercing of love—he calls her *daughter*. The world looked at her as an outcast, a misfit, unworthy—Jesus saw a beloved family member. *Daughter.*

Jesus had time to love her, precisely her and precisely love because he gave her exactly what she needed—dignity, value, attention. Being a Christian is difficult. How to be a Christian is not. It is laid out pretty clearly: Love God with all you've got and love people.[48] Which means, if you don't have time to love people, you can't live the Christian life.[49] You are a twin of this hurried world, and look, with each harried moment, less and less like Jesus.

Love is costly. Verse 35 shows this: "While Jesus was still speaking, some people came from the house of Jairus, 'Your daughter is dead.'"

First, can we mention the bedside manner here? Goodness. These are some rough friends. No manners. Not *I'm very sorry* or *Can you take a seat?* They don't even come with the good news-bad news construct: "The good news is you found Jesus! The bad news? Well, your daughter is dead. We're very sorry, but hey, this Jesus guy … wow, right?" No, they just pull the pin, hand the grenade over, and evacuate.

Jesus shrugs this news off, reassures everyone, and just keeps on walking. Not running, notice. Not anxious. Just walking toward whatever is next— the next right step.

That step led to another and another and eventually to a commotion. The house of the synagogue leader was in chaos, and Jesus met that storm as he always does, with stillness: "Why all this commotion and wailing?" He confronted the commotion with rest, renewal, and peace.

I wonder what you'd feel like if Jesus was on your team at work or part of your small group? What would be the feel of the group when his car pulled up outside? What kind of deep breath might be taken? And then I wonder what kind of breath my arrival brings? Is it one of relief or is it more of a here-we-go-again variety?

Jesus healed the girl, but even in doing so, his pace was different. He walked slow. He stayed calm. His pace was different because his perspective was. Jesus' perspective produced three key beliefs: 1) God is in control; 2) God will win; 3) God's victory grants eternity. When we say "yes" to everything, when we try to fix everyone, when we fixate on FOMO, we cannot be walking in those realities. Instead, we are making less of God's power, his sovereignty, and his call on our life. God doesn't sign off on a rushed YOLO life. No, he converts it, in bringing us an eternity, into a calm YOLOF life: You only live once, *forever*. It sounds like a Russian comedian, the Great Yolof. But with that perspective we don't have to rush. We don't have to hurry. We don't have to lament an endless bucket list that we won't have the margin to get to. We have forever! *Europe, I'm coming for you—on this side or next.*

Sometimes I speak at churches because they feel compelled occasionally to showcase a lack of discernment. Recently, I was onstage and through the spotlight could see, right at my eye level, a menacing red clock. There was another countdown clock on the projection screen at the back of the room in case I didn't take the hint. I could almost hear these clocks—tick-tock, tick-tock, tick-tock. This is the way of church. Shorter talks … tick-tock; fewer songs … tick-tock; be on time … tick-tock; move people out, move people in for the next service … tick-tock, tick-tock, tick-tock. And this is church! What about in our tasks, our jobs, our vacations; days, months, years … tick-tock, tick-tock, tick-tock. All our lives, we are nagged relentlessly by the sound: tick-tock, tick-tock, tick-tock. It is maddening. It is all we hear, as life has become an unceasing race, a tiring tick-tock time trial. We rush from one deadline to the next without noting the irony of calling it a deadline, for truly, our lifestyle is killing us.

This way of living has seeped into every area, including my marriage. It is in that realm that I had a realization that was apt for application in the other compartments of my life. It is best displayed by two trips to the grocery store.

Trip #1

I tell my wife I have to run to the grocery store. She asks how long I'm going to be. I say what we all say when such questions come our way: 15 minutes. Which is totally true if some sort of zombie apocalypse has taken place and no one is on the road. Which is totally true if there isn't a soul in the store other than the one checkout person who also happens to be the Employee of the Year. But I say 15 minutes, imposing a self-made deadline on this foray. "Oh, can you get milk and cheese?" my wife shouts toward my back as it and the rest of me hustles out the door—once more into the breach ….

And then I whip the car into the street, Mario Andretti style. No time for music—it takes my Bluetooth eight seconds to pair. No time for that. I drive fast … and furious. They should name a movie that. Or about 20. I take the most direct path. I take yellow lights as mere suggestions, pumping the gas at their appearance. Yes, I run a few "rellows." I race into the parking lot, and like a vulture, circle the coveted spot everyone wants. It will be mine. I make loops in the parking lot like Pac-Man on the really fast-mode, and I see a spot open near the door. I take it, cutting off a grandmother to do

so. She flails her hands dramatically; I tell her with my hand that
she is number one, as I sprint by her Buick and rampage into the
store. I snatch a shopping cart. It is the jank-wheeled one that pulls
left hard, but I am five feet away from the receptacle—no time to
make a trade. I'm off—supermarket sweep mode. I see a pregnant
woman drop a box of cereal, and I kick it under the shelf so she has
to struggle to reach it; gotta slow her down—she's eating for two,
after all. Can't risk getting behind her in line. I see a friend from high
school near the Gatorades, and I do what we all do with friends from
high school when the clock is ticking—I duck him, darting past like
I'm in Pamplona. I pluck items willy-nilly, paying no mind to the price
or health merits. I'm on the clock. I approach checkout aisle #7 but it
might as well be #13 because, unluckily, there are seven morons in
front of me. Don't they know this is my time to shop? Why don't they
open some other stupid lines? I'm surrounded by fools, and that is
when it hits me: milk and cheese! I forgot the milk and cheese. But
there is no time now, plus two more idiots have had the audacity to
get behind me in line. There is no going back. I take out my phone.
Stupid emails from the people I work with—do they have no concept
of free time? I check the news. Great, a tsunami in Japan, and now
I have that to stress over. Thanks, climate! I get on social media,
just to ratchet up some dormant envy. It works. Seems like pretty
much everyone's life is going better than mine. I have anxiety and
bitterness, and it converts to resentment, and all this inner angst
doesn't remain inner; no, it always finds a target. In this case, I look
up and see a teenage checkout girl who doesn't care nearly enough
about her job. Doesn't she know that I am late? Young people these
days. Back in my day we had some pride, some gumption. If I had
more time I'd talk to her manager and teach her a lesson. Finally,
in what seems like days later, I approach her with my goods. She
fumbles them and I will my eyes to shoot lasers, just this once. I

hmmph my discontent with a shake of the head, as I snatch my goods, before hurtling my misguided cart along. I hurl my groceries into my trunk, surely smashing the delicate eggs, a different type of tsunami. A storm of soul. I drive, drive, drive, cursing against the red lights and other drivers. Sweating, I arrive home, and nearly clip the garage door as I Tokyo Drift into the garage. I ram into my child's tricycle. Little chump must have been out while I was gone. How many times do I have to tell him to put it back where he got it? I rage from the car and slam the tricycle in its spot, wanting them to hear me inside: daddy's home and he's mad. I strap every plastic bag to my arms, veins sticking out, circulation gone, and head for the door. A bag breaks. Another complaint for the manifesto I will compose to the manager, if I ever find a spare two minutes lying around, like these damaged groceries at my feet. It has been 27 minutes and I burst into the house. My wife greets me with, "What took so long?"

And. I. Lose. It.

I do so through a three-day silent treatment, or maybe I explode with anger and tell her she doesn't know what it is like out there and that she can get her own groceries next time and good luck getting her own milk and cheese and that there was a tsunami in Japan. JAPAN!

And we sleep in separate rooms.

Trip #2

"Hey, honey, I'm going to the store."

"Oh, can you grab milk and cheese?"

"Sure."

"How long will you be?" she asks. The question ... and now the answer that makes all the difference ...

"I don't know. Maybe 45 minutes?"

I walk. Not out the door, over to her. I give her a kiss goodbye. I do the same with my kids—you never know when goodbye is long-term. Always make the time.

I start the car, take a breath, and wait for the Bluetooth to pair. Good music goes a long way. Into the mystic I go taking the scenic route. I like this route because there is a pasture with horses. I wave at the horses, hoping that someday one will raise its hoof and wave back. Taking this route adds an extra thirty seconds onto my drive, but I could come back with a story for life.

I pull into the parking lot. I chuckle at all the people competing for the same thing. I pull into the spots far from the door—the ones no one wants, a competition I get to always win and it comes with the consolation of no door-dings.

I stroll toward the entrance, taking note of the weather. If it is too cold, I'll be more thankful for the heat of the store, of humanity. If it is hot, nothing feels so good as the whoosh of the automatic doors and the air conditioning enveloping my face. Sometimes it is so refreshing I head over to the exit, leave the store, and do it again.

I select a cart from the receptacle. I notice it has a jank-wheel. Not today, Satan. I return it, testing a few more before I choose a winner. And off I go, into the produce section.

I don't need produce, but there is something about being that close to things that are so very close to life—their smell, their colors. It is good.

Down the cereal aisle, I see a pregnant woman has dropped a box
of cereal. I lope over and pick it up for her; placing it in her hands,
I ask how far along she is. No. I don't do that. Unless P-R-E-G-N-
A-N-T is tattooed across her forehead, I leave that alone. But I tell
her I hope she is well and exit the lane feeling good about helping
another person.

I see a friend from high school near the Gatorades. "Mitch!" I
shout. He doesn't move, probably doing what so many do when
they see friends from high school—ducking me. "Mitch!" I repeat,
approaching. "Hey, man! How are you?"

Mitch and I reconnect. As I engage him about his life, I notice a
heaviness—something is wrong. "Hey, man, everything okay?"

"You don't have time to get into it," he answers with a wag of the
head.

"Actually, I have about 19 minutes."

His head about explodes when I say that. We agree that the
Gatorade section is no place for a proper catch-up, but we trade
emails and intend to coordinate to have breakfast together soon. I
leave him better than I found him. My heart thrums with mission.

I near the checkout lanes when it hits me: milk and cheese.

I smile as I make my way to the back corner, willing to go the extra
distance for the woman I love. I am a good husband.

I approach checkout #7—how lucky!—and see quite a few people
in front of me. I don't count. I don't care. In fact, I'm delighted for the
rest. I breathe. I think about how clever the endcap is. They always
get me with the Tic-Tacs. I don't reach for my phone, knowing
boredom is also where rest lives. I breathe again instead and look at

the tabloid pics of Bennifer. People are interesting.

I glance at my cart and see the milk and reflect on the last time I milked a cow. That time is never because I live in a place where someone does that for me. All of this, I didn't farm or produce any of it. I will leave with a cart full of food and I will pay for it with money I have attained because someone pays me to do a job.

My heart swells with gratitude, thanksgiving, hope. Peace. And all this inner joy doesn't stay there, for it never does. It finds an external recipient.

It is then that I notice the teenage checkout girl working a job she doesn't want for too little money, and I remember what it was like to work a job I didn't want for too little money while my friends were off at the lake or on some such adventure. My heart swells with empathy and compassion for her. Is there anything so hard in life as growing up?

I approach when it is my turn with a soft smile. I catch her eye, as she fumbles with my items. "Thank you for doing this. This is a hard job, and I appreciate you."

I just birthed kindness where it didn't live before. I made, *ex nihilo*, goodness.

"I like your little blue vest," I offer as I take my things and mosey toward the exit.

I load my car with care, placing the eggs up front—"Precious cargo," I whisper to them.

I drive home the scenic route, I and love and you.

Pull gently into the garage.

I notice my son's tricycle is out. Park, exit the car, and take it up with wonder. I never thought I'd live in a house with toys and trikes and little tikes laughing and wrestling and playing. How blessed am I? I place it back in its place, in a manner that will make it easy for him to get to tomorrow.

I park and carry the bags in two installments.

I ease through the door.

It has been 29 minutes in this version. To which my wife offers, "Wow, that was fast!"

And then we make love in the kitchen.

The last part isn't true, okay? But it is my scenario, I can do what I want with it. The rest of the story is truth. I realized this one day when I was lamenting my work, my schedule, the sheer amount of meetings and commitments, and my sweet wife responded, "Can I ask you a question?" I nodded my approval. "Don't you make your own schedule?"

I do. And so do you. Perhaps not at work. Perhaps you have myriad demands on your life; I get that. But do you shower? What do you do in there? Do you have time for a deep breath, a prayer, in your various comings-and-goings? Do you have a desire to actually do something with that feeling of constant catch-up or do you secretly just like complaining about it?

Jesus offers us something else. He allows us to reclaim rest. To wrench rest into our regular rhythms. It is, after all, in his regular rhythm.

In the creation narrative, God creates a bunch of stuff in six days. And then on the seventh day, he rests. He sabbaths. It isn't because God is tired from juggling planets. He doesn't kick his feet up and think, "Self, I needed this." He rests out of goodness. Because rest is good and because he is good. He rests to model a rhythm so that we might follow that rhythm into that goodness.

When Jesus moseys on the scene, he offers this, "Sabbath is made for man, not man for the Sabbath." Meaning: sabbath is not some religious benchmark. Not one more thing to keep score on. Rather, rest is a soul necessity. A way of life. Jesus is giving a gentle nudge to be different and free by living different and free.

Christians place sabbath on Sunday. A good day to worship through song, through hobby, through naps. Naps! How good is God!? But also, believers need to secure a sabbath lifestyle, taking sabbath moments each day, each hour; I need to become a sabbath person. I need to breathe, a deep, mini-sabbath, a rest and renewal. This is a paradigm shift, but it is pinned to power, a power that promotes peace. Our biblical invite is to become a people, like Jesus, who operate from that position: one of deep soul-rest.

You should try it now. Here, I'll shut up ...

How long did you rest in silence? I hope if you didn't take a few seconds or minutes or hours, that you would. If it is helpful, just don't finish these last few paragraphs of this chapter. You've read up to this point—by now you know you aren't missing much! Just take a break. Take a breath. Ask God to restore life to your lifestyle. Embrace the quiet.

I love the passage in I Kings 19 where Elijah has been busy. He's been proclaiming and running and traveling and hiding from the authorities. The dude had some major stuff going on. Then this happens:

The Lord said, "Go out and stand on the mountain in the presence of the Lord, for the Lord is about to pass by."

Then a great and powerful wind tore the mountains apart and shattered the rocks before the Lord, but the Lord was not in the wind. After the wind there was an earthquake, but the Lord was not in the earthquake. After the earthquake came a fire, but the Lord was not in the fire. And after the fire came a gentle whisper.

God wasn't in the noise; God was in the whisper.

What might it be like to live in a way that we hear the whisper of God loud and clear? It would be different for sure; full of purpose and intentionality, a life lived closer to right—a life lived different from the rest because it is lived from a place (and person) of rest.

6. GODS

I was talking with a friend the other day. The door was closed, so perhaps our mouths were opened wider than they should have been. We were talking about another friend and a complicated situation. Later, when I assessed the conversation, it was confounding how it bobbed between gracious and gossip, like every sentence was a coin flip determining kind or cruel. It brought to mind *Jekyll and Hyde*.

Since it has probably been decades since you've read or lied to some teacher about reading the Stevenson novella, I'll summarize it. Jekyll is an upstanding citizen, smart and unremarkable. Hyde, meanwhile, is a mayhem-producing maniac. Jekyll knows Hyde, but can't control him. In the end—the big reveal—it is determined that Jekyll is Hyde; Hyde, Jekyll.[50]

The story comprises a wretched duality, and the same duality is alive in our hearts and on the pages of Mark 8. An important note about Jekyll and Hyde too: they die at the end. Similarly, the war within us leads to despair, destruction, and death.

It rages even now. You may doubt me because it is not monstrous. There are no popping veins or bulging eyes. This battle is sans contortions. Rather, it is sneaky, subtle. It is that niggling feeling that keeps you up at night. It makes life feel empty, hollow, and small. It numbs us from the vibrancy of reality—truly, it is a sort of unmaking. We are made to be a thing, a flourishing divine participant; yet we, instead, lead lives of quiet, longing desperation. In the novella, Jekyll takes an elixir to become Hyde. Until one night when no elixir is needed—he just transforms. Then in the daylight it happens again—Jekyll is helpless and hapless. As Hyde gathers strength, Jekyll is unmade.

An example of how this ravages quietly is that of a young man. He was raised in a religious family whose plan for him was to become a clergyman. The man, however, was more drawn to living things than lifeless prayers, so he struck off into the world, writing, collecting, gathering, and learning. His arrival home was an arrival, indeed, for the man was heralded as a genius. His works were published, and a lecture circuit commenced. He had become a somebody. Is there a drug more dangerous, an elixir more poisonous? For this man, it consumed him—he chased his next breakthrough, but it always eluded him. With each "failure" he delved into deeper despair. He spent the last 15 years of his life in a dark depression: he felt like a nobody. His name was Charles Darwin.[51]

That is the evolution of our own narrative. In social sciences this is sometimes called the Hedonic Treadmill.[52] That we are forever run-run-running toward some elusive goal or some mythical happiness, and both are always just out of reach. The notion of stepping off the treadmill is outlandish, and failure is not an option—stop and you plunge off the back of the treadmill. I must press on. Without ever-shifting success, life is not worth living.

Phillip Brickman is often credited with coining this phrase, Hedonic Treadmill. He knew it because he lived it. He died it too: Brickman hurled himself off the roof of a building adjacent to his university office.

The truth of it is this: life is killing us. Look around. We are discontent. Maladjusted. Unfulfilled. When those of faith see such a pattern, it is only natural to cry out, "Lord help us!" In Mark 8, Jesus answers: "Okay."

In verse 27, Jesus asks his disciples who people say that he is. He gets their answers, and then he does a thing that he usually does—he aims at the mind of the individual, plunging from the 30,000-foot view of things to the center of the heart. Peter answers, a thing *he* usually does, "You are the Messiah, the Son of the Living God."

This is a massive breakthrough. Up to this point, Jesus had been regarded as wise, a teacher, a prophet, one of many. Important but not ultimate. This declaration from Peter establishes a new title for Jesus: King.

In Matthew, we get a more robust portrayal, which culminates in Jesus saying of Peter's confession: "Blessed are you, Simon son of Jonah, for this was not revealed to you by flesh and blood, but by my Father in heaven. And I tell you that you are Peter, and on this rock I will build my church, and the gates of Hades will not overcome it" (V17-18).

If Peter didn't know it was a big deal, he did after Jesus said that. Catholics would later use this passage to lay claim for the idea of a Pope, with Peter serving as the first sacred leader of the holy church. Protestants say "the rock" is in reference to Peter's actual confession—the confession is the foundation, the rock in question.[53] Whichever interpretation one takes, however, we can agree that the confession is required—it is what prompts Jesus' words. And Jesus' words? They are the promise of a built church. Many claim to want a built church, but likely what they mean is that they want the church to be one more means of social scorekeeping, another setting on the Hedonic Treadmill. In truth, the built church always must have the Petrine confession as a foundation—that Jesus is, indeed, the Messiah. Without that at the core, it doesn't matter what a church's attendance is or if it has rich mahogany in its building. Without the confession, a church is just a vapid replica of the real thing and without any of its real power. For a built church, we must have a robust confession about the person and work of Jesus.

Regardless of interpretation, this passage is a big deal that shapes the rest of church history, yet Peter's version in Mark is pretty muted. Some claim this is due to Peter's humility, which seems a bit of a stretch knowing Peter's displayed character in scripture. It may be true, however, but it also may be muted because of what happens next in the story in Mark.

In verse 31, Jesus reveals his plan to the disciples. Now that they are grown enough to begin to see him as he really is, he deems them ready to digest the solid food of his plan—to suffer and die. This is not what Peter signed up for. This is some fine-print shenanigans, and in verse 32, he takes Jesus aside and "rebukes him." So one second Jesus is the one true king, almighty and able, and in the next breath he (according to Peter) requires a second opinion.

If nothing else, this is extremely awkward. What is Peter thinking? What is he doing? I can't believe he'd be so foolhardy to trust Jesus with the cosmos but not with the details. I mean, doesn't Peter understand the power and sovereignty of God? Who would do this?

And then I think about my Tuesday. Every Tuesday. And each Wednesday. And Thursday. Pretty much every day of my life I lament my lot in life. I should have more favor, more money, more talent, more opportunity, and less sickness, less pain, less challenge. Seriously, God, if you'd just consulted me beforehand, we wouldn't be in this mess, would we?

Well, we see Jesus' response to this via his reaction to Peter: "'Get behind me, Satan!' Jesus said. 'You do not have in mind the concerns of God, but merely human concerns.'"(V33). Ouch. Jesus calls Peter the most evil entity in existence. Deep burn, Son of Man. Deep. And the reason for the depth of this burn derives from making human concerns ultimate. Human concerns, in the world view of Jesus, are equated to a satanic/evil agenda when they are placed over against the will of God. We either follow the path of Christ or pursue the plans of evil. Through this lens, what happens to Peter (and us) becomes clearer—he hopped onto the Hedonic Treadmill.

Earlier we zeroed in on Darwin, but let us take aim at another biographical sketch. There once was a young man from a line of somebodies, and somebodies beget somebodies—it is a tale as old as time. As such, this young man was lined up with a big-deal job that would grant him power and wealth and influence. And to this job he said, "Nah, I'm good." This is a paraphrase. His actions spoke much louder as he abandoned his family in order to be an impoverished itinerant preacher. His family was used to having its way, so it forbade the young man from continuing this faithful farce, yet again actions spoke louder than their words—they kidnapped the young man and imprisoned him in their castle. This captivity went on for months, the family getting more and more desperate to bring their prodigal to his senses. To help with this, they decided to prey on one of those senses—the sensual. They hired a prostitute to lure him from his piety. Both he and the prostitute went screaming from the room—she running in desperation as he pursued her with a fire poker. Seeing that he would not acquiesce, the family finally did, releasing the young man to his own foolish designs.

For the young man, those designs became philosophical. He whiled the hours away writing philosophical arguments and theories about the existence and nature of God, and in so doing, he became great by accident. His name was Thomas Aquinas,[54] and despite his prestige he remained untainted by his fame because he wasn't running the rat race of the world. How did he remain somewhat pure, protected from the rigors of the treadmill?

In his philosophy, one of his ideas echoes the biblical narrative about idolatry. For Aquinas, there were four main idols—unrealities that put people on the treadmill.

The first of these idols is money. John D. Rockefeller gave perhaps the best interview answer ever when asked how much money was enough. His answer: one more dollar.[55] You are not the richest person on earth, like Rockefeller, so how much truer is his statement for you? Write down, for instance, how much money you make. Now write down how much money you would like to make or should make. I'll bet how much money I wrote down that the second amount of money you wrote down is more than the first amount. We thirst for a job that pays a decent wage, and then 50K yields to a desire for 60K. But studies show that it takes 80K to really achieve happiness,[56] so 60K becomes a desire for 80K. But 80K is so very close to that elusive six-figure income—so why not strive for 100K? And on and on it goes, an end that never ends. This is why joy and wealth are such rare companions.

Aquinas's second idol is power. This draws people—we want to be on boards, give our ideas, make decisions. Like Miranda's *Hamilton*, we "want to be in the room where it happens," and care very little about which room. This explains why there are so many "experts" online. Read a comment section about the tamest subject, and it takes about four seconds for the know-it-all bluster to start. This is also why we don't forgive others and love to take and hold on to offenses. Any time forgiveness is needed, it means one person owes another a debt. We withhold that forgiveness because we'd rather be god than be like God, who forgives freely and abundantly. We like the throne; any old throne will do. It is also for this reason that churches are filled with judgment. It is how people of faith keep score. Judgment is how we tell the masses that we have more points than they do; it is why so many sermons are preached to and about people who aren't in the room.

The third idol is pleasure. Ever stare up at a mountain with awed breath and begin thinking about the next mountain? *Wow, the Rockies are majestic ... I need to look into visiting Machu Pichu next year!* We become foodies to celebrate and consume great cuisine, and before long great cuisine is consuming us: time, money, energy, all bent on that next bite. Sexually speaking, the examples are too many to list—we crave more and more until the affair is fully launched, the fantasies in our head birthed into nightmarish realities, unsatisfying and unrelenting.

Finally, Aquinas lists fame as an alluring idol. In this, he was well ahead of his time. In fact, "fame" was such a futuristic concept by today's standards that the word he uses instead is actually "honor." Going viral wasn't a thing in the 13th Century. More recently, in the 1950s, children wanted to be firefighters—that was a popular vocation on elementary school surveys. Nowadays, kids list "being famous."[57] *Famous for what?* one might ask. The answer: it doesn't matter—just give me the fame! We make gods of celebrities, celebrities of pastors. Social media works to undo us, as we dance on TikTok and claim it is for the fun of it, yet we live and die by how many people view and like the personas which we project to an uncaring world. We crave to be seen, and whether we are really known or not, whether we are truly us or not, gets disoriented by the makeshift flashbulbs.

Ecclesiastes proclaims that eternity is in our hearts.[58] These four enticements promise a faux transcendence that is always just out of reach. Fulfillment comes after one more deal, flex, fling, or show. These moving targets are truly Band-Aids on bullet wounds; these moving targets make moving targets out of us.

This line of thinking brings slavery to mind. A good rational question to ask is: *How can anyone make a slave out of another human?* The answer is pretty simple: they don't. If some megalomaniac authored a course entitled *Slavery 101*, the first lesson would be to dehumanize the slave—make an object out him or her. People don't enslave people. People objectify others away from their humanness in order to justify slavery. It is the same process with sex-trafficking and even, at the base level, lust. You are not a human with dignity and personhood, but rather a collection of parts that will temporarily appease *my* longing. You are a means to an end, and that end is my fulfillment.

The idea of objectification is pertinent here because that is what evil does through money, power, pleasure, and fame. Evil uses those things to make objects out of us, to rob us of our personhood—we are mere objects, running legs, echoing Fitzgerald's line, "So we beat on, boats against the current, borne back ceaselessly into the past."[59] Only we think such effort will take us to some utopian future as we serve cruel unfeeling gods who care nothing of us and can ultimately do nothing for us.

Cancel culture understands this well. When a person is cancelled, it is the world taking some combination of Aquinas's four idols away as some form of punishment. You affronted the masses, so we will withhold your god. Cancel culture is, at its heart, spiritual warfare with gods of a different name. And what of the cancelled host or celebrity or politician? Do they see the removal of fame from their life as an opportunity at freedom? Does the removal of power free them from the very small room in which they've locked their existence away? No, when cancelled, when fame or fortune is taken from them, they twitch at the soul level, every thought on the treasured thing they lost and how to get it back. They have become versions of Gollum, forever striving to reclaim their precious money or power or access to pleasure or fame. They wretch and grope to get back on screen, back in power, back on stage, back to earning—borne back ceaselessly. Why don't they just stop? Why don't we? Because we can't. We are addicts in need of a fix.

Try cancelling Aquinas. The only thing left to take from him is his life, and his deep-rooted faith informs him that even death has lost its sting. It is for this reason that Christianity has grown in times and places of persecution.[60] Martyrs were stripped of all the gods of this age without even a shrug. Authorities tried to take more and more from these pathetic people, but they couldn't touch them at the soul level; they couldn't arouse the desperation nor darken the light of their eyes. So they took their lives, and the Christians faced the sword with songs of rejoicing on their lips. The truer the Christian, the less cancellable he or she is.

Of course, this is the rarity. The world is sick and its pestilence is wildly contagious. For those who follow Jesus, we dupe ourselves into believing this is an unbeliever issue, which is why this interaction with Peter proves so beneficial. It is likely here, as he jumps on the Hedonic Treadmill and focuses on human concerns, that Peter is a Christian. He's followed Jesus. He's given up much to do so, he's proclaimed Jesus the Messiah. He's been granted gifts of the Spirit in certain acts of service. One can quibble on the details, but all indicators point to Peter's identity in Christ by this point in the story. Yet Peter has these struggles, this temptation to test the treadmill. The reason he does this—and why you and I will too—is because this is precisely a Christian dilemma.

Think about what Jesus says to Nicodemus in John 3—that a person must be born again. That a new life begins and is to be fed and nurtured into maturity. Notice, nothing is said about the old, existing self. Yes, there are verses that speak to the old being gone, but these verses tend to be aspirational and process oriented. The truth is that the believer's life is the now/not yet reality of spiritual schizophrenia.[61] On the cross, Jesus won the war, trampling evil underfoot. That is true now, and yet there are battles still being settled and sorted. We take immense joy from the abundant life in Christ now, and yet we face myriad trials and encounter much suffering in this world. Even life—we have it now, and yet a physical death awaits all of us. The Kingdom of God has won the election in a landslide, and yet we await the inauguration to come.

This is the Christian concept of reality—this now/not yet. It is sensible, then, to apply the same to our very selves. Which is why Paul can say in Romans 7 that he does what he doesn't want to do and doesn't do what he wants to do. It is why Solzhenitsyn drops the mic by claiming that the line between good and evil runs through the human heart—every human heart.[62] It is why the epistle to the church in Philippi includes confidence "that he who began a good work in you will carry it on to completion until the day of Christ Jesus."[63] This would be a pretty lazy promise if the work was, you know, already completed.

In all this we have a couple of answers to the age-old question, "Why do Christians do bad things?" The first answer is exclusive: because they aren't Christians. In our society, and in others since the inception of the faith, there can be a social benefit in claiming Christianity. This is why just about every American politician vaguely alludes to matters of God and country or their faith-based upbringing or their membership in some local congregation or another. It is pretty amazing that so many American politicians love Jesus so much, especially when the cameras are on and they are in the Bible belt of the country. It isn't hard to see through, is it? Christianity in this country has been a power-making vehicle. We have celebrity pastors with million-dollar salaries, but even beyond the millionaires, we have the small-scale narcissist who'll take whatever platform he can get—and on a Sunday, the pulpit is the easiest platform in town to come by. It is for this very reason that Christianity stagnated when it became the state religion of Rome.[64] When everyone became a "Christian" it became difficult to distinguish the actual followers of Jesus. I wonder how many people pose as pious practitioners in countries where Christianity is illegal? Remove the hedonic rewards and suddenly the posturing stops.

The second reason is inclusive in nature—Christians err in issues of character because Hyde is alive in them. And Hyde is powerful. And we are bad choosers.

Every Christian will go the way of Peter—one moment confessing, the next denying. In a sense, this can be comforting. Rather than my own missteps leading me to death, I am covered by an unrelenting grace, mercy, and love. Reassured that no temporary lapse of judgment or character separates me from the love of Christ. It is said the dude abides; he's got nothing on Jesus.

And while I can take comfort that Jesus recognizes and forgives my human proneness to wander, I can't allow myself to get too comfortable with this arrangement. In my complacency, Hyde thrives. In the story of the Prodigal Son, the younger son demands his inheritance, jumping on the Hedonic Treadmill and chasing wildly after pleasure. Well, the money runs out—as it does—and he ends up tending to the pigs. Dirty and hungry, he consumes the pigs' food. Each day he waddles closer and closer to becoming a swine himself. At some point, to avoid that fate, he had to get up and limp home to his father and his father's provision. To avoid becoming devils, we must all do the same. The puritans got some stuff wrong (fashion probably being one). But one thing they got right was their emphasis on the mortification of the flesh.[65] We could take a note from that and strive to do the same.

Jesus says to Peter, "Get behind me, Satan," and then he gently teaches his disciples. Peter is there with him. I picture Peter, with his head down, eyes focused on his feet for shame. And then I picture Jesus, pacing as he teaches, taking steps nearer and nearer to Peter. Placing his hand on Peter's shoulder. Lovingly bringing him back to the fold, encouraging the Jekyll within to lick wounds and rejoin the fight.

Jesus' words in that teaching are that to follow him, one must deny oneself. Deny self? What does he mean? It is simple—deny money, deny power, deny pleasure, deny fame. It isn't that these are bad in themselves, but they are treacherous and damning when made ultimate. These are byproducts and we should use them, but we can never allow ourselves to be used *by* them. We must deny the constant impulse and strengthen the desires for better, choosing real treasure, transcendent power, eternal pleasure, and the fame of being seen, known, and approved by the God of the ages.

Jesus then appeals to the logic of the situation (in verses 35-36) in saying that the body is temporal but the soul is everlasting; we are not bodies with souls but souls with bodies.

And then comes a scary promise in verse 38: "If anyone is ashamed of me and my words in this adulterous and sinful generation, the Son of Man will be ashamed of them when he comes in his Father's glory with the holy angels." There is much we could say about this, but a simple summation would be that we'll be given what we want—what we desire most; what we love best. We can go on guzzling salt water, endlessly thirsty or we can drink deep from replenishing streams which flow with forever Living Water.

It is interesting to begin viewing life through this Jekyll and Hyde dynamic. Suddenly, my impulses and decisions seem clearer. And it is this clarity that makes what comes before this passage all the more compelling. In verses 22-25, there is this blind man. Jesus does what he does: "Then the man's eyes were opened, his sight was restored, and he saw everything clearly." He saw everything clearly, but even so, he can still close his eyes. He blinks. He can don a blindfold.

So it is with us. We've been given eyes to see, a vision of the world and the true path before us. And now comes the choice: Will I choose to be blinded by self, running endlessly till death? Or might I keep my eyes wide open, with a sight that declares louder than the alluring whispers of the world, "You are the Messiah. The Lord. The King."

7. JESUS

The other day we bought a kitchen timer. It keeps time. But really time ticks on either way, doesn't it? Generally, we all think about time frequently—how many hours we've worked this week, how many days until Christmas, how we never have enough time. Far less frequently, however, do we give thought to the isolated minute or even second—the tick, tick, ticks of life. Then you take a timer in your hand and suddenly you become aware.[66] Reality becomes fixed within the framework of those ticks now: how much time is left in your turn while playing that boardgame with friends, holding that plank during your workout, cooking a dish, living a life. We become aware, and with this awareness can come an urgency.

In Mark 8, Peter confesses/announces/proclaims to Jesus: *You are the Messiah!* This is a statement of willing belief that Jesus is the chosen one, the Savior, the King. And with this proclamation, a timer is wound—the pace quickens and the plot thickens.

The question that sets off these events is a question from Jesus: *Who do you say that I am?* This is akin to "On your mark, get set, GO!"

I wonder how you answer that question? My guess, if you are like me, is that you probably don't all that often. Perhaps year to year, you assess it. Maybe month to month. The pious among us take inventory week to week as we get cleaned up and attend church services. But what about belief within the tick-tick-ticking moments of life? Belief on a timer, chockful of

awareness and urgency? *Who do you say that I am?* and then the winding of
a timer, an unknown deadline in place.

The truth is most of us avoid the question and the timer altogether. We
hide behind reasons for unbelief, validations to keep pushing the business
of today off to some distant tomorrow. As Jesus dials his mission up a
notch, we get to witness several reasons for unbelief play out.

The first comes in the aftermath of Peter's confession. He says that Jesus
is the Messiah, and then he gets to hear more about Jesus. It is like taking
an online relationship to the in-person meeting and realizing this is not
the love connection you thought it would be—the person talks really, really
loud about private things in the restaurant or shows up with a service pig
or something (hopefully, one sans demons). Peter hears Jesus' plans to suffer
and die and feels like he's been duped by the not-so-fine print. With all the
cards on the table, Peter dislikes the way Jesus plans to play the hand, so he
takes Jesus aside for a good, old-fashion rebuking. Peter has a come-to Jesus
talk with Jesus. Which is odd. It is also embarrassing, sinful, and public—all
their friends witness this misstep. That public misdeed could certainly pave
the road for Peter's ultimate unbelief, just as our own foibles surely compel
us to walk hurriedly away from Jesus. Reason one for unbelief: You are
unworthy or beyond belief. Some behavior or action you've taken, some past
transgression, has put you beyond the reach of grace, of forgiveness.

This is where many of us live. The address: 143 Shame Circle—a dead-
end drive. At the heart of the biblical narrative is the idea that humans are
sinful. All of them. Including you. You are sinful. And beyond just being
sinful, pretty much all of us are worse off than we think. Consider all the
wrong you've done in your life, but now add to it all the good you've left
undone—every dollar hoarded, every encouragement held back, every
avoidance of serving someone else. Even those of us with self-esteem issues
still underestimate the besmirched state of our souls.

But this truth—that you are a wretched sinner—doesn't disqualify you from Jesus; rather it is precisely what qualifies his coming to you. *He came for you, sinner!* This is hard to fathom though, and even harder to accept. We think, *You don't know my addictions. You don't know the levels of my dishonesty. The anger I feel in my heart. My envy. My hatred.* Perhaps not, but Jesus does.

Once a coworker told me that she attended a Garth Brooks concert. She had last row seats in a giant stadium, yet she was happy to just get in the door. Before the concert, one of Brooks' staff approached her and her friend and asked if they would prefer to move to the front row. Apparently, there are a handful of musicians who do this—they don't sell the first few rows and then send staff people to the folks in the nosebleeds and offer them the best seats in the house for free. This is what Jesus does—he reserves the best seats in his house for sinners.

Peter has a few moments in the New Testament that should disqualify him from belief and certainly the right to be a leader of belief. Good thing for him (and us) that we are measured by Jesus' qualification and not our own.

If you feel secret shame, too sinful to follow Jesus, you actually have the first prerequisite for belief. *Congrats, you made the team. Varsity. Here's your letter—sorry it is cross-shaped. We're kind of a strange high school.* Jesus paid it all. Jesus is perfect. His invite is for our belief in him, not some bloated confidence in ourselves.

This is illustrated as we move along to Mark 9. In verse 2, Jesus tells a couple of his boys that they are going on a field trip. He calls Peter's name. I'm sure Peter thought he had misheard it. "Uh, don't you remember what happened like two paragraphs ago? You know when I sort of openly rebuked your plans as being moronic?"

Jesus is like, "No. No, I don't remember that." For Jesus takes our sins in his hand like a stone and hurls them into the sea.[67] He is all-knowing yet chooses to take our slights against him and remember them no more. "Let's go, brother," I picture him saying to Peter. And then Peter—can't you just see him galloping to follow, like my tiny kids when I say, "Who wants to go to work with dad today?"

Jesus is lovingly reminding Peter that the question is not *Who do you think you are?* It is forever *Who do you say that I am?*

The field trip they are going on is weird. We used to have to go to a farm once a year and watch a farmer milk cows and such. It was pretty strange. This is stranger. Jesus and a couple disciples head up a mountain. It is likely in the pre-dawn darkness, when suddenly Jesus lights up like a Christmas tree. In this state, he is joined by Elijah, the Old Testament prophet, and Moses, the Old Testament hero. Elijah doesn't always get the modern-day love because we like our anti-heroes—give us some flaws. We prefer David because he was a warrior with some lust issues and who is, at times, a moody musician. That is more our lane. Elijah is almost boring in his excellence. He is very likely the best non-divine human in the Bible, and certainly his face would make the Rushmore of faith in the days of Jesus. Moses is more familiar to us because we are forever drawn to freedom. Lincoln used politics and speeches to deliver slaves, but Moses got his hands dirty, walking the captives to freedom and then bounding around the wilderness of that freedom with them. He is the original great emancipator.

So, this trio is having their meet-and-greet when Peter pipes up, as he is prone to do: "Let's set up some tents!"[68] What? Are we going to make some s'mores? What's he talking about?

Linguistically, it is more likely that he said the word for tabernacle or temple, which is far more reasonable because the temple is where the glory of God was kept in the Old Testament.[69] There were specific ways to approach God's glory, and people had to be careful about it. Like the time Moses goes up on a mountain and God's glory is going to pass before him, but he has to hide and can only witness the back of the glory or it would be too much and kill Moses. When God's glory would manifest in some physical way, the term Shekinah Glory was used—a divine physical presence. Encountering this glory without the proper precautions would mean death.

This is what Peter is alluding to—the separation between God and humankind. There is a massive chasm between us and God. We stand there at the cliff's edge, looking at the promised land off in the distance; an endless darkness lies before our feet. It is on us to get back to God, but a step forward would be the end of us.

We all feel this, too, this separation. An old John Mayer song came on the other day. In it, he gives a rundown of things in his life: *Friends— check; Money—check; Well slept—check; Opposite sex—check; Guitar—check; Microphone—check; Messages waiting, when I get home—check.* Aptly, the song is called *Something's Missing.*[70] Indeed, something is missing.

And this is where religion comes in. Religion seeks to deal with the eternity we feel in our hearts, this longing for transcendence. It promises that if we clean ourselves up correctly, practice the proper rituals, engage the right mantras, that we can build a bridge across the void. It is like we leave the cliff and head back to the woods behind us. We fell trees and saw boards, and plank by plank, we begin constructing a way back, a bridge across the chasm.

Trouble is, this is hard. Bridge building is extremely laborious. Religion is, too. All the proper things in their proper places at the proper times, and always far, far, farther to go.

It is also dangerous. What if we do all this work—a lifetime of it—and then we fall? It could take one misstep, and we are right back where we began. Or what if we begin covering a chasm and discover that we've been bridging the wrong gap all along?

Religion is disheartening. It is hard to tell how much further we have to go, and if we are making progress, or enough of it. Because of this, religion becomes judgmental—my means of gauging progress and process is to assess the progress and process of others. Am I doing better than they are? Who is doing better than I am? Comparison consumes.

It is the religious mindset Peter is relying on when he suggests the tents/temple/tabernacle. His mind feels the gap between himself and what he is seeing before him on that mountain, and his answer is, "Let's cover you all. Honor you properly. Approach you the right way. Get a system in place. Let's get religious!"

But also something else is going on. Verse 6 is wonderful. It says, parenthetically, that Peter said this because he was terrified. I love thinking how that back-and-forth went between Mark (the author) and Peter (the basis for the non-fiction story):

"So then I said, 'Let's throw up some tents.'"

"Wait, what? You said what?" asks a befuddled Mark.

"Yeah, I don't know. He was glowing and Elijah and Moses were there. I dunno. I guess I was pretty scared."

"Okay, I'm definitely leaving that in there—'Peter was afraid.'"

This is the second reason for unbelief for many of us. Reason two for unbelief: You don't know what to believe and you are scared. Scared to get it wrong. Scared to admit vulnerability. Scared to get it right and it severs something from our lives; it brings change.

Often how this plays out is that our fear masquerades as doubt. Honest doubt propels thought and action. I saw this the other day watching a guy scurry up a tree to cut away dead limbs at my neighbor's lawn. Once up on the main branch, he tested his rope. Repeatedly. You could tell he didn't quite trust the rope—he had some doubts. So he threw a second rope to a different limb, and then proceeded with the work, gaining trust with the original rope as he swung from limb to limb.

Dishonest doubt is just our way of trying to make hiding honorable. For the tree trimmer, this is a mistrust of the first rope, and then a failure to complete the job—leaving with a claim of sickness or saying that the agreed upon wage is unfair or some other more noble excuse than being afraid.

Many of the common reasons for unbelief live in this realm—noble-sounding excuses. Like Africans. I've encountered easily a hundred people who claim a disbelief in Jesus because of the African who never hears the gospel. This strikes me as nonsensical for many reasons. First, can you tell me the name of this African who is the object of such devout compassion? Second, have you looked at heat maps of Christianity? Africa is white hot with gospel fervor.[71] It is likely that there are a bunch of African holdouts to belief for the fears about the Westerner who never hears the gospel. That fear would be more justifiable. Then there is the whole geographical reality—that Africa is actually nearer the starting point of the Christian movement than the ends of the earth where the concerned person, typically with a Starbucks in hand, is sitting. My response to this person has usually been to consider world hunger. If a person is concerned about those in the world without enough to eat, the answer would never be swear off food forever. No, that would mean death. Concern for the hungry would compel a person to eat a good meal and get busy trying to use resources to make sure others can, too. The same line of logic goes with truth—a thing is true or it isn't. If it is true, your adopting it, promoting it, and supporting it will only make that truth more audible. Adding to suppression is not a cure for a suppressed notion.

Another of these claims is that a person doesn't believe in Jesus because there is slavery in the Bible. There is also slavery in every generation in recorded history. So by that standard of evaluation, Aristotle is cast out; Newton with him. All philosophy of every age is tainted because it was wrought forth in an epoch containing societal moral blight. Of course, the same would hold true for our own age as slavery and sex trafficking are still, sadly, alive and well. Every age is tainted by sin—that doesn't invalidate the Bible for it is precisely what the Bible claims. And as for slavery, the Bible never condones the practice, but it does describe it via the cultural norms that accepted the heinous practice. In fact, Christianity is built on an anti-slavery premise: love your neighbor as yourself.[72] This is a chain-breaking mandate if ever there was one.

We could go on listing these "concerns," but I think a youth pastor had the best take on it. He would send kids from his youth group off to college, and then, in the summer, he'd get to go have lunch or coffee with them. Many of them would head off to university, claiming a belief in Christ, but would return recanting that faith. When out to coffee with these individuals, the youth pastor would listen to lofty ideals about African tribesmen, slavery in the Bible, suffering in the world. He'd listen patiently, and when the self-important lecturer would stop for a breath, he'd ask a single question, "So, who you sleeping with?"

Fears about complexity or change or vulnerability or restrictions on the things we want to do force us into hiding. I play hide-and-seek with my son who is scared to go into any unoccupied rooms of our home. So he ends up in the living room, with half his body clearly visible. He'd rather be dull and safe than explore the wide-open unknowns of the house entire. Even if in that safety, the game is lesser.

Who do you say that I am? asks Jesus. "I'm really scared to say," comes our timid response.

Up on the mountain, God speaks. Then, Elijah and Moses are gone—I have them fading like the images in the photograph ala *Back to the Future*. And then, just like that, Jesus comes down the mountain.

This is easy to miss, so I'll just run through the situation one more time. Jesus is called the Messiah, a distinction he doesn't push back on at all—the chosen one. Then Jesus is spoken over by God, *nbd*. All of this while he is glowing—glowing! In a few instances, light is a symbol for the Holy Spirit. If that is the case here—and it may not be—that would mean all three persons of the Trinity make an appearance. Added to that are the greatest prophet and emancipator of the Old Testament, who both give Jesus hugs and hand-pounds of approval. And then Jesus is home for dinner. He walks down the mountain. Once more, Jesus is with humankind—the physical manifestation of the divine, the Shekinah Glory; there walking amongst the people, laying hands on them, washing their filthy feet.

Remember the chasm we spoke of earlier? We approach the cliff's edge and stand pondering: *How do we get across? Which morality or religion is the best bet to traverse the great expanse? How do I even make the bridge? Is there even enough time to get there?* All the while the timer is tick-tick-ticking away.

And then—a figure appears in the distance. Coming close, close, and ever closer. Like the disciples just know it is Elijah and Moses up on the mountain, we just know this figure who approaches is Jesus; we feel it with every fiber of our being. He arrives, making it all the way to us—he's built the bridge from the other side! He's come to us. He's come for us. He's made the way, with splinters in his carpenter hands; he stops a step away, clears his throat, and asks, "Who do you say that I am?"

Jesus and the disciples head down the mountain. They arrive to a hubbub as religious leaders and the remaining disciples are fighting about a sick kid. Pretty odd thing to fight about, honestly. The disciples have attempted to heal the boy and the teachers of the law are pretty stoked about their failure in this, "Haha! Suckers! He's still just as sick as he was!" They proceed to touchdown-dance over the boy's seizing body.

While these teachers are explicitly moronic here, the disciples are only slightly better. They, for their part, at least tried to heal the boy. But both they and the religious leaders neglect the power and provision of Jesus. Neither believes enough to trust or to act with this power. At the end of the passage, Jesus reveals to the disciples, "This kind of evil spirit comes out with prayer." *Oh, prayer! Totes forgot that, Jesus!* This is analogous to the modern church, which spends hours and hours on rehearsals, planning meetings, budget sessions, yet cannot find a spare second for prayer. With our strategies and initiatives and savvy leadership, we've dismissed Jesus from our midst—"We can take it from here, Lord. Thanks for coming. Godspeed." Then, as we stand around singing worship to ourselves and all we've built, we wonder why no healing is happening.

This makes evident a third reason for unbelief: You don't believe because you don't need belief. Is there any phrase so utterly freeing as, "There is no god"? With this declaration, the untethered soul is unbound by the chains of religion, and, in this state, this faithless person flees the bridge altogether, running for the dense trees of the forest—there the potential wonder, the transcendence, is safely hidden from view. *Thank God (or lack thereof)! Freedom!*

But then a curious thing happens. The yearning remains. That something missing feeling is inextinguishable. For all the dismissal of religion, the person of unbelief becomes religiously political. Or, if not politics, then, say, musical. I know someone who loves music, but that isn't enough. They now must love music more than any other human on earth. *You went to six concerts this summer? That's cute. I went to 67 shows last night.* Perhaps the religious tendencies skew toward art or just social contexts—ruling the neighborhood, any old neighborhood will do. Point is, we can't help it. Religion seeps into the groundwater of everything. We lap it up unknowingly. We worship; we approach—makeshift gods of a different name. There is always another chasm; it's just whether or not there is transcendence on the other side. Far too often we get over there across the money bridge or fame bridge or drones bridge or six-pack-ab bridge (I've heard about that one, but never experienced it firsthand), and it just feels sort of empty, much like it did on the other side. And all the while, the whisper of that original bridge remains. It woos. It calls. But the timer ticks on—our life is but a mist, a vapor. Will there be enough ticks left to find the bridge and cross?

Similarly, with time in mind, Jesus asks a time question in verse 21: "How long has the sick boy been like this?"

His father's answer reveals another reason for unbelief. "Since childhood," he answers Jesus.

Now, it is unlikely that the father is willing to cause this sort of fracas to bring his son here to the disciples on his first attempt at finding a cure. Can you imagine this sick boy turning 12 and the father saying, "Well, Timmy, I know you asked for a healing, but instead I got you this pony! We can consider healing when you are a bit older."

It is possible that the man was just waiting around and heard about Jesus and took action. More likely, however, is that the man had tried a bunch of stuff. Over-the-counter drugs, Eastern practices, various religious mantras. I would wager that he's tried a couple spoonfuls of remedies—all the boy's life this father has been searching and seeking a solution. That is what love does, how hope moves.

It is also another reason for our unbelief in Jesus: You believe in other things more or first. Science. Education. Morality. Humanism. These things just need more time, more funding, the right leader. I sometimes wonder if the reason we can never find that perfect leader is because he's already been found? He's been standing at that bridge waiting for us all along—calling to us through science, in our learning, through the moral laws we live by, in and through the human spirit and the fact that we look and live a smidge like our Heavenly Father.

The man asks Jesus, concerning his sick son, "If you can do something …"

Jesus meets the phrase with a rhetorical flex, "If you can?"

This is like us asking: *Can you take me across the bridge? Will it hold our weight? Is it any good over there?*

Jesus' answer to us and the boy's father is the same: *Do you believe?* Or said another way, "Who do you say that I am?"

The father responds, and so do we. But we invert his answer. Our answer, in our Western academic world is, "I unbelieve, help me with my belief."

We lead with unbelief. We do not trust Jesus with the tick-tick-ticks of our life, but we give our very souls over to our untried doubts.

Growing up I doubted eggs. I doubted eggs because my father had a taste aversion to them. Even the smell would sicken him. This doubt led me to a hatred, an aversion all my own. Until I turned 18 that is. Then belief broke through and shells with it—I tried eggs. I don't know if someone told me it was a rare type of candy or something, but I put some scrambled eggs in my mouth, and it was my eyes which were opened. I ruined like 39 pans that summer, scrambling eggs. I had more omelets than Waffle House. My problem was never eggs; it was doubt. For 18 years, I never once doubted my doubt.

We do this all the time with people. We dislike a person based on body language at one meeting or social interaction. We foment a low-grade hatred because the person frowned at that one wedding reception from across the room. Based on that one isolated instance the person is dead to us. But really it was the doubt that killed. Most of the hatred we have for people in our lives would dissipate over a single coffee meeting, especially with those in our churches. But instead, we just go on feeding the flame of furious hidden hatred.

The same thing happens with Jesus. We had that one creepy priest in school or knew the obnoxious Christian (or the other one). We had to watch bizarre religious shows growing up or went to a camp where we had to braid each other's hair while confessing our sins. Just like that, from some strange or hateful standalone experience, we come to doubt Jesus. We throw baby Jesus out with the bathwater. Faith isn't perfect, so we don't want it, another reason for our unbelief: You don't believe because your faith is imperfect.

Yes! That's right! The bridge of faith we've been mentioning, well, it is really high. It is scary up there. The wind blows. The distance is hard to gauge. Yet, with starts and stops, we trudge along, one step at a time. One step at a time. A plodding, forward progress. One step at a time.

This one time I was in a Bible study. Some people were Christians, some were not. I was the sole person in the group in semi-vocational ministry. As such, the leader liked to use me as a prop. On one occasion, he asked me in front of the group, "So, Matt, what percentage would you put on your belief?"

I wouldn't, is what I wanted to answer, and probably, after hearing my answer, what he would have preferred me to say. Instead, I went with this gem, "Well, I dunno. On a good day I'm somewhere in the 80s. On a rougher day I'm probably in the 60s. I'll call it 76 percent."

His chin almost hit the table—I was supposed to be his bastion of belief! The patron saint of the group! Every two weeks I cashed a check in Jesus' name, *Amen*—how could I dare not be 100 percent?

Well, because life is hard. And I am finite. And God is perplexing. And large. What I want is a faith that allows for growth, accepts mystery, and trusts both to capable cosmic hands. Again, I've come to lean on

Philippians 1:6, which says that he who began a good work in me will, "carry it through to completion." That means it isn't complete yet! He does the work, progressively, and I can trust his work. Or there's that passage where Jesus says that with the faith of a mustard seed that he can move mountains.[73] We fixate on juggling mountains or something—*Look at us! Look at all this power!* More so, we should focus on the wry face of Jesus who looks at something so tiny, this miniscule seedling of a thing, and says, "Yeah, that'll do! I can work with that. Have you seen my other work? I mean, this mustard seed is huge compared to the normal *ex nihilo* I usually create from!"

The timer of our lives will not wait for perfect faith. Not enough ticks. By this man's reply and Jesus' response to that reply, Jesus doesn't demand perfect faith.

"I do believe, help me overcome my unbelief" (verse 24).

This is honest. True. Beautiful. And instructive: We can believe with our baggage, unloading it as we follow Jesus. We can believe with honest doubt. We can believe that in our belief, Jesus will work; that he will help us overcome ourselves and this world.

Jesus' response? He heals the boy. Protects him. Then lifts him to his feet. I wonder what that boy's feet would do when he came to the bridge of faith? If he'd doubt and dawdle? I wonder what our feet will do as we stand at that sacred precipice?

The timer ticks on. But at some point, for all of us, it won't. We stand before the bridge of belief and the time ticks on, closer to its finish, a tick closer to the end of this moment, of this sentence …

All our life, the ticks parade, a progression toward finality, and with each one, Jesus stands before each of us and asks, "Who do you say that I am?"

8. ANGER

Mark 11 features a greatest hit. Most people know about baby Jesus, Jesus on the cross, and then Jesus back-to-life. Outside of those tracks, this is the next one to make the jukebox, or, to use more modern language, to get spins. Here, let's download the scene together:

The next day as they were leaving Bethany, Jesus was hungry. Seeing in the distance a fig tree in leaf, he went to find out if it had any fruit. When he reached it, he found nothing but leaves, because it was not the season for figs. Then he said to the tree, "May no one ever eat fruit from you again." And his disciples heard him say it.

On reaching Jerusalem, Jesus entered the temple courts and began driving out those who were buying and selling there. He overturned the tables of the money changers and the benches of those selling doves, and would not allow anyone to carry merchandise through the temple courts. And as he taught them, he said, "Is it not written: 'My house will be called a house of prayer for all nations'? But you have made it 'a den of robbers.'"

The chief priests and the teachers of the law heard this and began looking for a way to kill him, for they feared him, because the whole crowd was amazed at his teaching.[74]

Yes! Finally! I read about Jesus walking on water or him stilling a storm. I've tried both. At once. I was told the pool was closed and I needed to wear swim attire next time. I went home all wet. Born a virgin? *That ship's sailed.* Water into wine? *Would have been nice in college.* Heals a leper? *I don't even know a leper.* Jesus is told that he is the Messiah; I'm just a mess.

But finally, in this scene, we have a flawed Jesus! Jesus gets hangry and throws a tantrum. *I can do that! WWJD! Let's go!*

When he was three, my son got into the Incredible Hulk. Or at least he got into an Incredible Hulk costume; he had no contextual knowledge of the hero. He'd also wear the little green muscle suit and insist we call him Mr. Hulk, which I thought was paradoxically mannerly for a rage-maniac. Adding context, Bruce Banner is a nerdy, unassuming character whose alter ego, the Hulk, eats rage for breakfast. That seems to be what goes on with Jesus here. The Prince of Peace loses his religion and Hulks out.

I want to consider that more but begin by acknowledging that we fail with passages like these because we have a dysfunctional relationship with anger. For half of us, we see Jesus using anger and think: *See! I told you I'm allowed to yell-and-stagger about the house/lawn/neighborhood!* This is the passage we crochet on pillows—maybe that is the origin of the term "throw pillow"?

The other half of us, well, we are a little embarrassed by Jesus' actions here. We clutch our pearls and think, *Well, I would never! If Jesus would just attend the conflict resolution seminar at my workplace. Doesn't Jesus know about avoiding triggers? Maybe he should pack a Lunchable for the onset of the hangries?*

A friend told me the other day that she had never seen her parents fight growing up. Which means she had to become an adult before she really ever saw adults resolve conflict—conflict that she was now a part of. Her story is common. Just as common, though, is the rest of us, whose families regularly resembled episodes of *The Jerry Springer Show*.

With that in mind—our dearth with dealing with anger—I want to lead block with two ideas. The first: Anger is ... good.

In America, women can vote. People of color also vote. When it comes to slavery, the United States has become decidedly against it. What do you think about that?

Well, if you are a rational human being who honors dignity and decency, you are pleased with these realities and are probably perplexed by seeing them brought up as if there was ever even a question about them. The thing is—there was a question about them. For a long time. And here's another question concerning them: Without anger, I wonder if women or people of color would have the vote? Without anger, I wonder if we would have abandoned the treacherous human blight of slavery? At some point, someone got good and angry about these things. Others joined and the fight for justice was on.

Anger has been on the forefront—the spark—of undoing corrupt systems since history has been recorded. One can find hieroglyphics depicting the banishment and battle over rulers taking the lion share (literally, perhaps) of food from the mouths of the people. Anger stands up to Hitler, topples Mussolini. Anger marches for equity and equality and personhood. Anger revolts, persists, dreams, and pursues. Anger stands and kicks in the door of sex trafficking. Anger yells *STOP!* to drunk driving. I love that a group that has made immense progress against drunk driving uses the acronym M.A.D.D. These mothers were good and mad about burying their school-aged children.

Anger, in some ways, is a gift of God because it is a part of God. It is part of God because God is love.[75] And part of love is anger: the love of dignity provokes an anger at injustice; the love of personhood, an anger at objectification; the love of the oppressed, an anger at oppression. I love my kids to the point of anger about them running out into traffic. I love my wife with an angry ferocity at any who would demean or abuse her. The

Bible is full of God's love, shown in God's anger. Anger at destructive sin—at his children running into spiritual traffic. At his bride being seduced and violated by a villainous suitor.

There are beautiful verses which claim that God will fight for his people.[76] That the God of the cosmos would go to war for you? Goodness, we follow a good and angry God of love. A God who does not sit idly by when evil occurs. Anger is God's forever reaction to injustice. It prompts his pursuit at having justice roll down like a mighty water,[77] and flows forth from his unceasing love of goodness.

For us, well, we are made in God's image.[78] We possess a sense of the divine in our being. Therefore, there is a type of anger and ensuing action that is good and acceptable.

Paul speaks of this in Ephesians when he says, "Be angry, yet do not sin. Don't let the sun go down on your anger."[79] This follows three chapters of theology and is the section of the missive extolling believers of Jesus how to live. We are told to choose the transformed self—to put it on (much like selecting Jekyll from chapter six)—so we can take Paul's approach at anger to be part of the transformed self. Paul doesn't say, "Don't be angry ever!" because Paul doesn't mean that. He doesn't mean that because, contrary to what some Christians have come to espouse, anger isn't sin.

God is angry in the Old Testament 455 times (and that is just what the Bible records!). Several of those unspoken times are mentioned in Psalm 7:11. I favor this verse mainly for its reference: 7-11. It brings to mind the convenience store, which, in the heyday of convenience, became available longer than competitors, from 7 a.m. to 11 p.m. Eventually, that even was outdated and a 24-hour approach was adopted—night-shifters need hot dogs, too, after all. So Psalm 7:11 is a perfect reference to speak on the frequency of God's anger: "God is a righteous judge, a God who displays his wrath every day." Every day. Open late because evil doesn't rest. Like a sense of hunger prompts eating, a sense of anger can prompt meaningful action.

This idea—of anger being good—makes some people uncomfortable. Especially people who live with those who are making photocopies of this precise section of the book. "Guess what I read today, honey?" they'll say zealously between breathless tantrums. For those people, let's add a second point: Anger is … bad.

Earlier I mentioned the delayed suffrage of women and people of color. I brought up slavery and its inferred brutality. I again wonder about those things, but this time query how much those broken systems were caused by misplaced, repressed anger—irrational anger toward women or minorities? And where it isn't the cause of such things, anger surely perpetrated and protected abusive practices. It was the anger of the controlling male or slaveholder which held virtue at bay.

Via anger we beat ourselves, our spouses, our children. Physically, verbally, mentally—seldom a day passes when I don't commit some form of murder in my heart. Proverbs 29:11 says, "Fools give full vent to their rage, but the wise bring calm in the end."

Anger is bad because it is misused, with bad anger being a byproduct of power and control. Traffic around me should part like the Red Sea because I esteem myself more important than the people around me—my schedule is the priority, the demands I need to meet, commitments I must keep. You'll notice this in organizations, like businesses and churches: as individual power increases for a leader, detachment will occur for that leader who simultaneously becomes more and more prone to fly off the handle. Angry pastors and CEOs and coaches and superintendents persist because they feel they must protect their precious power and keep their cherished control.

Anger is also misapplied. Brené Brown has a great video in which a cartoon version of herself reenacts a time when Brown dropped a cup of coffee on the floor. Her immediate reaction was, "Damn you, Steve!" Steve is not the name of her hand—which dropped the coffee—nor the moniker of her favorite mug. It is the name of her husband, whom she blamed for this incident because it was her second cup of coffee, which she wouldn't be having if Steve had not come home 30 minutes late the night before.[80] And Brown is supposed to be good at this stuff—to have a handle on it, even if her mug is now handle-less. But she isn't always great at this because none of us are—we act out of anger that is disproportionate, selfish, and irrational. And we do so at the people we love most as well as strangers, and youth sports coaches, and baristas, and coworkers, and mall Santas, and television script-writers, and hapless authors who drone on with examples, and … you get it because you've got it: anger issues.

Winston Churchill is credited as saying, "A man is about as big as the things that make him angry." He's half right, for the quote applies for women too. The next time you want to throw your phone or remote control because something isn't loading fast enough, consider the quote and what universal hardships cause us vehement reactions.

Aristotle takes a softer approach: "Anyone can become angry—that is easy; but to become angry with the right person, and to the right degree, and at the right time, and for the right purpose, and in the right way, that is not within everybody's power, that is not easy."[81]

Anger, then, is a mixed bag, and we must be careful with it, knowing our anger by knowing our hearts. But with anger two basic choices present themselves.

The first of these choices is to let it go. Now, this isn't in some Stepford Wife sort of way. Christians especially can fall into this plastic Zen exterior, fixed smile plastered on face, chaos raging within. No, letting anger go is not the same as pretending anger doesn't exist. The biblical term most in line with is idea would be forbearance. It is in the family of forgiveness. When we engage this option, we acknowledge our anger, and, for the believer, we join this acknowledgment to prayer. Something like this:

I am angry. I see no positive course of action. God, take this situation. Take this anger. Safeguard me from resentment. Give me peace.

Your version may sound different, and it is likely this isn't some one-and-done statement—it isn't some magic wish. No, it becomes a mantra that we may need to repeat to God and to trusted confidants or a journal. We may need to revisit this prayer and the situation that prompts it in appropriate times and seasons. Like if the initial affront is familial and comes during the holidays, well, one had better make this meditation as ritualized as decorating the Christmas tree.

A friend has some family members who are hoarders. What they hoard is befuddling, for what they horde is trash. It began in the kitchen: they just wouldn't take the trash out. When the kitchen got full, they formed a second trashcan out of the guestroom. That is what many of us do with our hearts when it comes to anger. We just keep storing it away, and, like this person's house, it begins to smell, to have associated problems like pests and rot; eventually damage gives way to destruction.

My wife called me at work and began with, "I'm really mad." My initial thought was, *What did I do now?* Though, if you know me at all, *What did I forget to do now?* might have been nearer the mark. By God's redeeming, all-powerful grace, it wasn't me this time! Rather, it was an incident at the playground. At the time, my oldest children were ages four and three. Out on a late-summer day, they frolicked and bounded and rejoiced in the sloping joys of the slide. Only that is where the trouble started—there were three fourth graders holding court there. They began calling my kids "nerds." Honestly, they probably weren't wrong. But still, it was hurtful, and this was potentially my sons' first time being picked on by other children in this way. The mama-bear in my wife activated and she told those boys that they were "being mean." She needs to spend a bit more time with the Hulk, it would seem.

This went about as expected—the boys began making fun of her too. They added curse words into the mix, for good measure, and went from annoying to intolerable.

"What can I do?" she said, seething into the phone.

"Well, you can't beat them up." I responded.

"I can take them," she reassured.

"No, I know. Yes, you can probably take them. But I've just never seen beating up kids going all that well for adults. Just seems like a failed strategy."

"I could talk to their parents?" she suggested. "They are sitting on a bench nearby and totally oblivious."

"Well, yeah. But if they are oblivious and their kids are cool with cussing at preschoolers, they may sort of always be oblivious. Also, I doubt they take the side of the frazzled park lady over their precious cherubs, you know?"

"Yeah," she said, flummoxed.

"Here's an idea." I didn't want to strand my love on this island. "I can leave work and swing by the convenience store. I'll buy some cigarettes. Then I'll go to the top of the slide and teach those boys how to smoke. Their parents will smell the smoke, come over, and berate me that their children aren't old enough to smoke. To which I'll reply, 'Yeah, and my children aren't old enough for curse words, so I think we all learned a little something about each other and life here today, wouldn't you say?'" I waited to get the go-ahead from my wife, keys in hand. After quite the silence I said, "You still there?"

"Yeah," she sounded defeated. I guess I'd have to save my idea for when she was out-of-town sometime.

What we ended up saying at the end of the conversation, our gameplan, was this: Sometimes we lose. In life, in faith, in this world—sometimes we lose. Every fight is not our fight, and to be on-crusade about everything all the time ... well, that is no kind of life. So that day I said this:

I am angry. I see no positive action. God take this situation. Take this anger. Safeguard me from resentment. Give me peace.

I don't want to carry this along. I don't want to hate all fourth graders forever and become the get-off-my-lawn guy. And if I'm really feeling the Spirit and wanting to honor Jesus, I'll add to that prayer, *And be with those boys. Help them. Guide them. Love them.*

I am angry, and when I choose to let that anger go, I have to let it go somewhere. I choose to give it to God.

The second course of action is to take positive, reconciling action on the situation causing us anger. This is not the lesser option, nor is it always the harder option. It is just a different option, and some steps will help inform us which road to take.

The first step is to acknowledge our anger. A starting point in this is to recognize the injustice that has taken place. If we cannot find any injustice, then our anger is just a form of selfishness, and we need to seek help in dealing with that, while giving the anger over to God. Jesus recognizes injustice that day in the temple courts. For starters, the temple was being used as a shortcut. There were hundreds of thousands of people in a town with ancient-world infrastructure—so crowds aplenty. But in using the temple as a thoroughfare, it was also a shortcut to opportunity. Merchants set up booths, exchanging currency at a deplorable rate—similar to what mall ATMs used to do on withdraws when I was in high school. I'd head to the mall to buy some candy or something and attempt to withdraw $20. The fee would be, like, $25. High school me would run the numbers and think, *Yeah, that seems like a pretty fair deal and it would be a perfectly wise fiscal decision for me to proceed.* People in the temple courts needed Jewish coin for sacrifice and were being up-charged on the conversion of their Roman money.

Speaking of up-charged, have you seen the prices on nachos at ballparks? It is the same practice that these merchants were employing here at the temple. Many people would come to make a ritualistic sacrifice—out of faith or superstition—of doves. That's right, doves. You know what gets flagged going through TSA every time? Doves. You have all these travelers in town, none of whom BYOD-ed. So the price for doves was ridiculous, and they didn't even come in little plastic baseball helmets either.

This whole thing was a massive scam—but wait, wait, there's more! The location of the scam, I think, is what sends Jesus over the top. This was all occurring in the Court of Nations, the place for outsiders to draw near to God. In the inner areas—the place for true followers—the religious elites were doing their religious things, unhindered by capitalistic endeavors. They allowed this and profited from it occurring in the *more* unseemly areas of the temple—you know, the sections for the sinners, the riff-raff.

People coming to approach God were being bilked, an attempt to diminish the glory of God. Jesus' whole ministry was marked by people being able to freely approach him. You might not always like what Jesus says or does, how he convicts or calls, but sick or lowly, poor or rich, good or bad, come-on-down, you are the next contestant on the *Price is Right.* And that right price? Well, it is free. It always is. Or at least it is supposed to be. When we create barriers of entry, we actively fight against God's glory and the practiced way of Jesus.

Jesus sees all this and says, "I'm angry!" Now, I don't know if he said it aloud, but I know this, you aren't Jesus so you should. There is power in naming a thing—this is why we confer names on our children, and why we feel such relief when a doctor can give a name to a malady or pain. Naming a thing bestows a sense of purpose and power. When we name our anger—call it what it is—it helps us know what we are feeling and what we are up against. I don't know if accidental anger ever works out for anyone.

After we acknowledge our anger, we should assess it. This can be tricky, especially for someone seeking to apply the Christian ethic to proceedings. On the night Jesus is arrested, for instance, Peter takes out his sword, ready to roll. Jesus stays his hand—he has Peter put his sword away. Or there is Jesus' famous teaching on turning the other cheek—get hit on one cheek, present the other. It would seem, then, that Jesus advocates for Christians always giving their anger to God and moving along. But let's consider this thought experiment: How does Jesus' teaching on turning the other cheek change if it isn't your cheek? Let's say you are standing next to an orphan and someone comes up and strikes her cheek. I don't think Jesus says, "Turn the other cheek, bystander. Let the orphan suffer. Count your blessings and move along." No, I think Jesus, in that instance, would say, "Go on! Stand up for that orphan! Stand in the gap for her! Love your neighbor as yourself, and your pint-sized neighbor just got accosted! Don't just stand there—do something!"

So here's the point—a way of assessing our anger is considering at whom/what we are angry and for whom/what we are angry. Often, when I'm angry, I'm angry about *my* time, that *my* car was damaged, that *my* reputation was harmed. Everything centers around me. In the temple tantrum scene, Jesus was angry *at* the religious people in power and *for* the lost folks missing out on God. Jesus' focus isn't on himself, but on his Father's house and name. Meaning if what we are truly mad about has self at its center, it is likely our anger needs to be acknowledged, let go to God, and that we seek out the root causes for this anger and challenge the selfishness that has embedded itself in the soil of our heart.

Applying this can be tricky. Suppose I'm upset about my kid's playtime in soccer. I ask the questions: at whom and for whom am I angry? My answers are that I am angry at the coach and I'm angry for my kid. My kid! A mere child! A supple being! An innocent! *Onward Christian Soldier* parades in my heart—I am justified to gossip about the coach, to call and confront him, to bring healthy post-game snacks for the kids as a display of my discontent.

But am I being honest? Is the playtime really about my kid (who, frankly, doesn't want to play soccer in the first place)? Or is it about me? About living vicariously through my child. About college scholarships. About having other parents admire me and compliment me so I can act all humble and say, "Gosh, I know he's great. I really don't know where he got such speed, good looks, and precision from …"

It is comical when applied to youth sports—even though it really happens. It becomes more dire when we apply this sense of gussied-up anger at things like activism. We post a lot on public forums, get bent out of shape, yell, and rage, when it really isn't about the lost or the marginalized or the innocents. It is really all about us filling some void in our lives, addressing some vapid need for attention.

Motives for activism which stand in stark opposition to the action of Rosa Parks. We all know it—1955, Montgomery, Alabama. Rosa Parks sits on the bus, but when a person of a different race boards, Parks is asked to move to the back. She refuses.

Her civil disobedience galvanized and fueled the Civil Rights Movement, which yearned for a rallying point. That day, Rosa Parks had had enough—that day, she got angry. But was she thinking about the movement? Was she thinking about how this incident would look on Insta? Was she thinking how she might garner a fame for herself which could carve out new opportunity? Nope. She was tired from work. Hungry. Sick of perpetual injustice. Hers was an act of angry virtue with fame as an accidental byproduct. An answer to a question about her desired legacy suggests as much: "I would like to be remembered as a person who wanted to be free and wanted other people to be also free."[82] Rosa Parks was angry at systemic racism and angry for those who lacked basic freedoms and dignity.

We have to assess our anger and make sure it isn't just about us, our temporary feelings—that anger isn't something that is just happening to us. Rather, our anger should be a tool we, by God's power, steward and control. James instructs people to "be quick to listen, slow to speech and slow to become angry."[83] Proverbs 16:32 says, "Better a patient person than a warrior, one with self-control than one who takes a city." Or elsewhere (Proverbs 14:29): "Whoever is patient has great understanding, but one who is quick-tempered displays folly." We are to control our anger, and often that is a question of pace—can we slow the circumstances and our feelings down?

Pushback to the idea of slow anger could be this very scene of Jesus in the temple. He flipped tables! Surely, that is not the picture of a slowness of anger—the guy just lost it. Well, except that he didn't. Look at Mark 11:11: "Jesus entered Jerusalem and went into the temple courts. He looked around at everything, but since it was already late, he went out to Bethany with the twelve." Jesus did a recon mission before the he flipped the tables—truly turning the tables on how we view this passage. Maybe he wanted to best use his anger in front of a bigger crowd—make more of a difference? Maybe it was late enough that many of the moneylenders were already off to the taverns or something? I'm not sure. But what we can be sure of is the sureness of Jesus' actions: they were considered.

This isn't new for Jesus either. At the beginning of his ministry, he brings the thunder in the temple as well. John 2:14-15 reads: "In the temple courts he found people selling cattle, sheep and doves, and others sitting at tables exchanging money. So he made a whip out of cords, and drove all from the temple courts, both sheep and cattle; he scattered the coins of the money changers and overturned their tables." Notice the middle—you know, the part where he made a whip! Jesus didn't roll in there Indiana Jones style. I also doubt that he had his handy-dandy whip-making kit at the ready. So this means he was angry, and then he sourced the materials for a whip, likely telling his disciples in order to help him procure the necessary leather. Perhaps he was having these conversations with the disciples, explaining himself, but whether or not he was talking, he was certainly thinking. Processing. Choosing action. I have him whistling a tune for the 15 or so minutes it took him to braid the leather for the whip. Jesus didn't, then, fly off the handle; he took the care and time to make the handle.

Another pushback to delaying the action of anger—taking the time to assess anger—may be the aforementioned verse from Ephesians. You hear this one used all the time at marriage conferences and the like, "Don't let the sun go down on your anger." I wonder how the people who teach folks to stay up all night fighting would take Paul if he were to instruct, "Don't count your chickens before they hatch"? Would those folks run out and buy a bunch of eggs, and be very, very careful not to know how many they'd purchased? Maybe they'd shop the poultry section blindfolded? More likely, they'd know Paul was using an idiomatic expression to make a point, the same way we turn phrases for impact. In Mark 11, we see Jesus purposefully letting the sun go down on his anger so he could execute said anger better in the morning. What Paul is saying, then, in this verse, is not to stuff your anger. Deal with your anger. Be wise with your anger. Work together to love well in your anger. Sometimes that means refusing sleep and staying up all night to contend and solve a problem. More often—because who among us actually fights better when tired?—it will go more like this, "We're angry. Want to get some sleep, wake up fresh tomorrow, and hash this out over hash browns?" That is no less a biblical approach.

In the assessment of my anger, I'll decide whether to let my anger go or to choose meaningful action. I should take some things into account. Like, what is the size of the infraction? When my four-year-old spills Fruity Pebbles on my lap before work, my reaction cannot be the same as when he runs out into traffic. That is confusing parenting for both him and me. Some wrongs are called slights and must be viewed as such. Christians should rejoice in slights. We should delight in the slight. For these are simple opportunities to showcase love and grace and forgiveness—to promote peace.

 Along with the size of the infraction, is the consideration of relationship— how well do I know the object of my anger? If my own kids are holding court on the slide, cussing at younger children and their mothers, they won't taste ice cream for a year. It is not going to go well for them, okay? But if I don't know the kids doing this, there isn't much I can do. My rule is this—if you don't know the kid's first, middle, and last name, then you can't punish that child.

Last, you need to reflect on the reconcilable actions which are available to you. I recall getting pretty angry at the writers for season eight of *The Office*. What? Was I going to drive out there? Were they going to read my angry letter and change their comedic stylings? "Whoa, guys, we need to reshoot season eight entirely at massive cost because Matt from Missouri is unsatisfied." I had a boss once say that each of us only has so many tokens. Spend them wisely.

After my anger has been acknowledged and assessed, I can pursue action if that is the wise route. When pursuing that, my target is not getting a pound of flesh. Nor is it flexing. It's not even winning. My target is reconciliation via understanding. Reconciliation can also mean change—repentance. And understanding might apply to the person who wronged me, but it could also refer to my own understanding. I have to leave the door open that I make mistakes and do not read every situation (or most situations) perfectly. So a loving conversation of conflict might begin with, "Can I talk to you about something that made me feel angry?" I think *feel* is an important word because we are not our anger. Then, I unpack the situation from my vantage, closing with some form of "What am I missing?" This last bit allows for the person to correct my misunderstanding, fill in a blank, give me the rest of the story. Often this information is vital and allows a perspective that mitigates the initial anger. We might have been missing something crucial, and now we can move along.

In the scene with the money changers, Jesus hoped they would change and that the temple leaders would repent. He hoped others would have unhindered access to God. The thread of our hope, in conflict, should run the same. And this, for us, operates best when love is led with—when people can be seen and known and loved, in the type of relationship that yearns for collective righteousness over individual rightness. It is the type of community the church is supposed to be.

Finally, after anger is acknowledged and assessed, and action is taken, we invite restoration and reconciliation. For the Christian, this should be made as easy as possible. That is not to say this comes without consequences or boundaries in place. Instead, it is to advise that this entire construct is built on grace, not punitive vendetta. If a person in my life wrongs me in a way that also comes with a 10-year prison sentence, I don't have to bust them out of prison in my gracious forbearance. But I also don't have to add another five-to-ten in some personal relational prison upon their release. For most of the minor conflicts in our lives, we should strive for a hug or handshake or prayer as sufficient means at restoring relationship, making grace abound in and around us. Romans 12:18 says to live at peace with everyone if it is possible and as it depends on you. These two caveats are thrown in, indicating that the Christian is supposed to go above and beyond to do his part, and sometimes reconciliation just isn't in the cards on this side of the ledger. In that case, we go back to the beginning of the process, acknowledging our anger and giving it to God.

Anger exists when God's glory is obstructed. Christians, then, ought to be the angriest people on earth. But before some Hulk "amens" that statement, Christians should also be the most tender with that anger. They should be committed to outdoing one another in honor, in respect. They should be immensely wise with their anger. And they should be peacemakers. Christian anger doesn't go around starting fires; it fights them, making God's will done on earth as it is in heaven.

This passage begins with a fig tree. The tree looks full and vibrant, yet it bears no figs; it is fruitless. Jesus curses it and it dies. But in truth, it was already worthless in its fruitlessness. As much as anything else, this passage, like that tree, is about the fruitlessness of empty religion. The Jewish leaders had a packed temple—the church was jumping. It showed all the signs of fruit, but it offered nothing of any value, of any worth.

So it is with us when we obstruct the glory of God in any way. For them, it was the barrier of commerce. For us, all too often, it is the barrier of toxic resentments, personal grudges, gossip, and abuse. This misused and misapplied anger hinders access to God for ourselves and others.

There is much to draw from this popular passage, but a simple takeaway is that we can trust Jesus to overturn the tables in our lives—to curse our fruitlessness because he loves us as children. But, just as much, we can, by that same power, live in a way, rooted in deep relational wisdom, that bears fruit where we've been planted in every season. We can use and process righteous, loving anger to produce human flourishing for God's glory.

9. POWER

What's the point of *Romeo and Juliet*? Not a question you were expecting today because you are no longer a junior higher in Mrs. Becker's class. But what would you say? Some would posit it is that we shouldn't judge a book by its cover—or a person by name (what's in a name and all that). Others might suggest that discourse matters. I mean if the Capulets and Montagues could have just, like, had a game night or something. Just get together, play some charades, and talk, this whole other charade plays out differently, right? Maybe the point is that love conquers all or that love conquers all *absolutely*. Could be the point of the play is that friendship truly matters or that wisdom is crucial or that patience is a virtue. Could be a lot of things, and, for that reason, if I was really pinned down by the question *Which is it?*, my answer would be *yes*.

Before pressing into Act II, though, let's consider for a moment the fact that I just invoked a play from the late 1500s. Even so, nearly all of us have a reference point to draw on. At the mention of *Romeo and Juliet* we have synaptic segues to reading the play or lying about reading the play or acting it out awkwardly in high school or seeing a movie version with a fresh-faced Di Caprio or jamming to the killer soundtrack from the Baz Luhrmann cut. The point is that humans are drawn together by stories because humans are drawn *to* stories. We tell them, watch them, even dream them.

Speaking of dreams, in *Romeo and Juliet*, Mercutio says, "True, I talk of dreams, which are children of an idle brain, begot of nothing but vain fantasy."

He nails it. This is the frustrating thing about trying to recount a dream. Life lesson here: no one wants to hear about your dreams. Sure, they say "yes" when you ask them if they do, but they are just being nice. No one in this life or the next wants to hear about your fantasy draft strategy, your explanation of why you lost a board game, or about some dream you had. They just don't.

How this plays out in my house is I ambush my wife while she is brushing her teeth in the morning. "I had a doozie of a dream last night," I quip. "Want to hear about it?"

Since she is in full scrub mode, she says nothing. I take this silence as her way of saying, "Yes! I thought you'd never ask! Please, tell me all about your dream from last night lest I die on the spot."

Always the obliging husband, I launch in: "Well, there were these crabs. They weren't regular ones, though. They had roller blades for feet. Well, some did. Others had wings. Anyway, we were in my high school, only it was actually Bayside High from *Saved By the Bell*, but still somehow my school in the dream. You were there, I think. But it wasn't really you; it was, sort of like a version of you as an animated vixen. And there was this storm, but instead of rain, it was a bunch of frogs all singing ragtime and then …." I notice my wife's dead eyes glaze over, much like when she was the animated vixen ignoring me in my dream.

We are drawn to stories but don't want to hear about dreams because dreams are pre-baked stories—they need more time in the oven. Mercutio calls them, "More inconstant than the wind." But great, developed, tethered, pull-out-of-the-oven-warm stories: they captivate in their constancy. While fixed, their meaning can be wide-ranging and far-reaching.

The Bible is like this. Especially stories involving Jesus. In much of what Jesus says and does, there is a fixed centrality yet wide-ranging application and interpretation: it is a casserole of layered truth-upon-truth, piping hot. Throughout the Bible, there are major and lesser things which form a Christian first, followed by a Christian ethic, or vice versa.

Picture a target. At its center is a bullseye—the star-crossed lovers' notion, the main point, the moral of the story. While the bullseye is the ultimate objective, there are other points on the board too. They may be lesser, but they still add value. This is how much of scripture is—meaning is a circle. If some takeaway is on the target, it adds value and matters. And it matters more and more as it inches closer to the center, the primary meaning, the bullseye.

With this target on our mind, let's throw a few darts pertaining to a single conversation with Jesus, eventually making our way to the bullseye at the center that holds the whole thing together.

The action picks up with Jesus' opponents forming an all-star team. Several groups jockeyed for power among the Jewish people, and while they were usually disunified and committed to generational in-fighting, a single thing had finally brought them together—they all hated Jesus. The goal of this newly formed alliance was "to catch Jesus in his words."[84]

A gaggle from this group approach Jesus and say, "Teacher, we know that you are a man of integrity. You aren't swayed by others, because you pay no attention to who they are; but you teach the way of God in accordance with the truth." This is funny. *Teacher? Teacher!?* Like 10 minutes ago these same people were calling Jesus *Satan.* Suddenly, he is some Yoda-like figure— *wise and measured he has become.* This could be an arrow on the target: be careful how you walk. Flattery should pretty much always be a warning sign of impending danger. The reason we come under the spell of flattery, ignoring the pitfalls prattling words predict, is that flattery corroborates with our pride. Our pride is secretly informing us that we deserve better, that we are better. So then someone else comes along and says the same sentiments we've been secretly nurturing and our confirmation bias rejoices—*now we're getting somewhere! Finally, someone recognizes how awesome I am!* Pride laps up flattery without realizing its poisonous qualities. But Jesus wasn't swayed by syrupy words. He is humble, the suffering servant. Because of his humility, he knew their hypocrisy.[85]

The question they come with is this: "Is it right to pay the imperial tax to Caesar or not? Should we pay or shouldn't we?"[86] It is a gotcha question worthy of yellow journalism or modern-day clickbait. The question places Jesus between a rock and the Colosseum. Rome is the ruling empire, regarded as the Empire is in *Star Wars* or as the British Empire was viewed by the American Colonies. *We don't want to quarter your stormtroopers and we don't want to pay your taxes!* Aside from loathing Jesus, this is the other thing all the factions trying to trap Jesus had in common—they all wanted Jewish liberation and independence. Therefore, if Jesus sides with Rome in any way, he is Benedict Arnold and he'd lose any foothold with his people and followers, the Jews. If he demeans Rome in any way—especially concerning the all-important issue of money—then he'd be messing with the man. His door would be kicked in and he could become a meal for lions.

This reminds me a bit of American politics during the Donald Trump administration. People hate Donald Trump, or they love Donald Trump—there seems to be very little middle ground. One reason for this is that Donald Trump is extreme. He was extreme as a celebrity, as a candidate, and as President. So then, when President Trump would say or do something unconventional—or when something surfaced that he had done prior to his presidency—his fellow Republicans would get cornered by political opponents. "What did you think of the President's comments/actions?" they'd be asked. If the Republican politician in question would denounce the President, their own party would turn on them, abandon them. If they didn't denounce the President, they could become complicit in a cause or conduct they don't condone. Take this scenario and multiply

it tenfold and throw in some barbaric implications, and you are close to the
circumstances Jesus found himself in.

In that moment, Jesus does what he always does—he breathes. Presented
with panic, Jesus is calm. "Give me a coin," he says. Taking the coin in his
hand, he inspects it.[87] He sees the face of Caesar, looks over the inscription,
and then flips it back to them and says, "Give back to Caesar what is
Caesar's."

A first arrow we could shoot at the target of meaning is this: pay your taxes.
That isn't the main point, mind you. But it is on the board for this passage.
The Bible is clear that followers of Jesus should be honorable citizens, even
when they occupy places and societies that are dishonorable. If one finds
himself surrounded by murderers, it does not grant him permission to
murder. This call to be civil citizens means our obedience to the mandates
of the societies where we've been placed rises to the level of worship.
When I drive 34 in a 35, I'm forsaking the manic need to arrive 18 seconds
sooner by driving 40. Instead, I'm setting the cruise control of my heart on
things above, on God and his honor; in simply obeying the speed limit, I'm
seeking first the Kingdom of God over the need to build and to control my
own kingdom here on earth.

The Bible is rife with examples of this, sans the automobiles. Nehemiah,
for instance, is cupbearer to the king. A king he didn't vote for and one
with foreign gods and disparate morals. Nehemiah rose to be one of this
king's top assistants, a confidant. Which created the perfect opportunity
for Nehemiah to sabotage the king. He could put whoopie cushions in his
throne, spit in his wine, undermine him. Nehemiah could spread rumors,
gossip, and even plot coups or an assassination. But Nehemiah didn't do any
of that. Instead, he served the king with skillful excellence. In Nehemiah 2,
Nehemiah approaches the king for a favor and greets him with, "May the
king live forever." Did Nehemiah really want the king to live forever? Did
he somehow buy that the earthly king was immortal? No, he was merely

addressing the king in the fashion of the day. He was paying the king respect and honor per the cultural mores of that society.

A few paragraphs back, I invoked President Donald Trump. It was a lackluster example and I considered cutting it. The reason I left it is because I wanted to say *President* Donald Trump. And then I wanted to double-down by saying *President* Joe Biden. When President Trump was elected, a lot of people took up the phrase, "That's not my president!" Then, when President Biden was elected, the same people who were mad at people who said "That's not my president" when Donald Trump was elected began using the phrase when President Biden won the office. Whenever I hear anyone say it, I want to respond with, *Can I see your passport?* or *Oh, yeah? What's your address?* Because the thing is, if you live in the United States, that *is* your president. Far too often, Christians have been content to let their political leanings be known by their *ad hominem* attacks, by their disrespect. I want, in God's name, to be known by what I love, to disagree charitably, to fight for justice but to do so fairly. This was not the king Nehemiah chose, but it was his king, nonetheless. So he paid his taxes. In this case, the tax of civility and service.

The same can be said of Daniel and of Joseph. They faithfully served rulers, with whom they had fundamental disagreements, as worshipful submission to God. And while we can find examples like this littered throughout the pages of scripture, they don't really address the more common citizen—the one who is not in direct servitude of a king. Fortunately, Jeremiah swoops in with his famous letter to the Israelites living in Babylonian captivity. They were captives in one of the most hedonistic societies that has ever existed. Every night was a Jay Gatsby rave—this place made the roaring twenties sound like a whimper. And the Israelites were keeping their distance, attempting not to get tarnished by all the corruption flitting about. From God, Jeremiah writes this:

Build houses and settle down; plant gardens and eat what they produce. Marry and have sons and daughters; find wives for your sons and give your daughters in marriage, so that they too may have sons and daughters. Increase in number there; do not decrease. Also seek the peace and prosperity of the city to which I have carried you into exile. Pray to the LORD for it, because if it prospers, you too will prosper.[88]

This had to be jarring for the Israelites. They thought civil separation and civil disobedience were the only acceptable courses of action, but God had a more difficult path in mind: civility. Building houses meant they were staying awhile—*get that 30-year mortgage note, settle in.* The Israelites complained about their heathen neighbors, but they sure didn't mind taking handouts and consuming these heathens' food; they lambasted their culture with provisions spilling out of their mouths. To this, God says, *Contribute! Plant some food. Start some businesses. Get a job.* He's calling them to do this and to increase—to influence the society. But the most unsettling part had to be when he tells them to seek the prosperity of Babylon and to pray for it. *What!? You mean we aren't just supposed to grumble on social media? We actually have to be salt and light?* And I love the not-so-subtle reminder God places in the instructions: "of the city to which I have carried you into exile." Sometimes we think God dropped his cellphone or something under the seat while driving. He takes his eyes off the road to fetch his phone or whatever, and when he looks up, he is shocked to see he missed an exit. God is bemused and must figure out some way of getting back on course. Reality is, God's hands are firmly on the wheel always—he carries us and history along, in perfect control.

We are to be good citizens, and the reason is the bullseye of Jesus' Caesar interaction. But before we come to that, let's chuck another dart, fire a second arrow.

Jesus is content to render to Caesar what is Caesar's because power is a paradox. Money is power. *He who has the most toys … wins.* Caesar has the money. His face is on it. Literally, a heady play by Caesar. Fame is power.

Caesar is an icon! Money is the thing that everyone wants to possess, and in that possession, they get acquainted with Caesar. More people of that era would know Caesar than Jesus, and it wouldn't even be close. If Caesar were to walk into a room, everyone in the joint would *Hail, Caesar.* If Jesus were to walk into the same room a few moments later, Caesar would have to inquire who Jesus was. *Who?* he'd question, channeling his best Michael Bluth, needing a last name that still wouldn't do the trick.

Caesar had money. He had fame. Yet Jesus is not moved or swayed by this … again. We see a similar mindset play out when Jesus is led to the wilderness to be tempted in Matthew 4. Hungry, Jesus is wooed by Satan to turn the stones into bread and sate his appetite. Jesus declines, so Satan tries another tactic, challenging Jesus to do a magic trick to display his great power. Jesus again refuses, and Satan saves the best for last. Taking Jesus to a lofty vantage, he offers Jesus all the splendor of the kingdom, the empire—all the power. All Jesus has to do is bow before Satan and Jesus would be made ruler; Jesus could *be* Caesar.

Jesus decidedly says *No.* The reason? Power is a paradox. Jesus would rather stoop to conquer. He would win the war by washing feet. He would die to live. The power of this world is weak and ultimately futile. It is like how I feel about my kids playing house—it is cute but ineffectual.

Jesus challenges the power structures of this world, but we don't quite trust him. Think of the church and this world. Begin with the world. It has a tried-and-true system of building worldly success. First, one must develop a product—something to sell. Second, a persona must be crafted to sell that product. Then, that persona is polished and promoted. Finally, it is time to cash in and repeat.

Throw ancient Rome into this recipe. Its product is Roman rule. Rome can build the best buildings, engineer the best roads and routes, and, when push comes to shove, it has the mightiest army the world has ever seen. All the world should look on at her splendor and chant: *Rome! Rome! Rome!* But to sell that, Rome needs a persona. *Hail, Caesar!* He will be the mascot for the mighty empire, the enduring image-bearer of the eternal city. As long as we can get his face out there, that is … *Currency!* Slap Caesar on every coin in the empire and all the world will know. Shape his jawline like JFK's on the half-dollar; give him an aquiline nose; bestow a nobility on that sacred image. And now, without further ado, cash in: tax and flex. Should this Caesar not do the trick, we have another waiting in the wings—just send Brutus and his boys in to carve out the details.

Applying the framework of worldly success to the Rome of Jesus' era, I coarsely just described modern marketing, how the booming influencer industry works, the inner (and outer) workings of celebrity culture. Modern-age branding is not all that different from ancient-world strategy—the mediums may have shifted, but the methods remain intact, which is why President Richard Nixon, when asked by a presidential hopeful what it takes to get elected, answered, "Lose twenty pounds."[89]

Along with describing the worldly construct of building success, I also just outlined the way we attempt to manufacture church in the Western world. Our product is a pseudo-Jesus, a sort of self-help guru with seeker-sensitive leadership advice. Our product is a slick church with a pristine campus and state-of-the-art technologies. Our product is attractional, flashy programs—*our kids camp this year will be on the moon!* Our product is a network of influence in our towns.

And to sell that product? We need a pastor. If we really get desperate, we can settle for a worship leader. This person has to be inspiring, full of charisma, active, innovative, visionary, organized, dependable, above reproach, talented. They will be our CEO, our king, our Caesar, our god!

But first a little polish and promotion. Let's get some hair plugs, frost those tips, dress him up like an Express mannequin—*Express is still cool, right?*

Find out if Express is still cool; if it isn't, find out what is! Let's get *Pastor* doing some roundtables, showing up to community events, speaking at conferences, recording 14 podcasts by lunch. *Book deal(s)!!!!*

And if he does everything right and all the walls glimmer just enough, we'll be able to cash in: Money. Size. Buildings. Influence. Programs.

My kids play house and we play church. Jesus looks at us and similarly says, "It's cute but ineffectual." A big, full building isn't fruit. It is just a crowd. And the answer is not what we do with the crowd—that mentality is part of the problem. The answer is what we do *as* the crowd. A church is a crowd transformed to community.

In Acts 8, there is this guy called Simon the Magician. *The Magician* is not his last name though that would be pretty slick; it is his vocation. He levitates on the strip. Makes rabbits bounce out of hats. Disappears skyscrapers. You know the type. Well, he comes to believe in Jesus, and then he sees a trick that blows even his magical mind—the apostles are healing people by the power of the Holy Spirit. He approaches them—*now for my next trick* dancing through his mind—and asks how much. How much would it cost to be able to do that—he tried to purchase the power of the Holy Spirit.

That is a picture of us. We think with enough money God will move. With enough wit or production or volume or the hippest service or most strategic capital campaigns or the most pristine buildings that we can claim our rightful power. We have crafted a copycat celebrity culture[90] all about personal preference and persona when church is supposed to be about pursuit: A God who first pursues us, and now, we, collectively, pursue him back—in service, in submission, in sharing, in love. Instead, we say things like, "Church was good," whittling down our spiritual pursuit to a passive rating based on preference. No, God was good. God is good. God will be good. He's the main event and the everyday feature—He's the icon.

In 2022, the Queen of England died. The funeral and surrounding events
and drama were quietly covered by every news medium on earth, non-
stop for a week. As I took in some of the reporting I remember thinking:
Every celebrity dies. Some while they are still alive. A modern storytelling convention is the "Happily Ever After" tagline. It used to end
our fairy tales, but now it has infected how we think about celebrities. A
truer statement would be "Happily Ever After … Till They Died." I'm
thinking about proposing those two statements to my wife for our his/hers
tombstones. When we tie our spiritual pursuit to the power-conventions
of the world—to product, persona, and polish—it will be happily ever
after until it dies. And it will die. At the next scandal or financial crisis or
when a leader gets cancelled. That's the thing about *Romeo and Juliet*—it
is a seemingly sweet tale that ends in death, becoming a runaway tragedy.
When we cling to the Caesar-structures of this world, we attach ourselves
to death. *He who has the most toys … dies too.*

But if I cannot cling to the systems of this world, what else do I have?

That leads us to the bullseye of the passage. In verse 17, Jesus says, "Give
back to Caesar what is Caesar's and to God what is God's." Not only is this
a brilliant answer, but it begs the question: *What is God's?* The answer to
that question is the arrow that pierces the heart of the matter.

Jesus' answer: *Everything.*

When a person believes Jesus, God changes that person from an earthly
citizen to a citizen of heaven.[91] Which means, if I believe in Jesus,
everything changes—I am freed.

Take my recent trip to Sonic, for example. I wanted the cheese curds they
have because, hey, I can't live forever. But they had raised the price. They
were 30 cents more than they had been. I got tater tots instead. Now give
me a billion dollars. With that in my bank, it would no longer be sensible
to nickel-and-dime my way through a Sonic order. In life, God owns

everything. Every dollar—and everything else—is his. And I am too. He owns everything, and that liberates me from nickel-and-diming my life away—from making everything about the money I have or money I lack. Money is moved from center; God displaces it.

If I'm a citizen of heaven, the politics of this world no longer consume me either. Because God is sovereign, I can join with The Avett Brothers in singing the lyric, "When your life doesn't change by the man who's elected."[92] God is not losing sleep over the state of the world, so neither will I. He is sovereign and I trust him.

If I am a citizen of heaven, the tactics of this world no longer control or compel me. I no longer need my church to give me some experience or else I'll leave. I don't need my money's worth from some Sabbath marketing firm. God is the experience, and I humbly get to share that experience with a community of fellow citizens.

If I am a citizen of heaven, I am liberated from the systems of this world. And with this freedom? Peter discusses this very thing in a letter he writes after Jesus leaves this world.[93] In it, he renders to Caesar what is Caesar's in submission to God. It isn't really about Caesar or the king or the president—Peter chooses to submit to the authorities of this world because they fall under the ultimate authority in his life: God. He goes on to speak of his freedom and concludes that this freedom is to do good through respecting people, loving the family of believers, fearing God, and honoring the emperor—even when the emperor is wrongheaded. Per Peter, Christians are, because of their freedom, to be fountains of respect, geysers of grace. They are unbound from this world and liberated to pursue the path of peace.

Paul echoes this sentiment by declaring death to have lost its sting.[94] The main point—the bullseye—is that death is no longer a fearsome prospect for the follower of Jesus. But on the target is the reality that death is the single worst thing any of us goes through. It is the lonely road we all must walk—full of mystery and doubt. Nothing else is as challenging as death, the ultimate hardship. Therefore, logically speaking, nothing else can sting either. Politics can be complex, hurtful even, but even political failure pales in comparison with death. When I see that my bank account is not where I envisioned, and it is unlikely to ever get there, it may kill worldly dreams, but it is nothing compared with actual death—so it, too, loses its sting.

Render to Caesar what is Caesar's—his wealth, his fame, his power. Because, in the end, he's God's Caesar. That is the bullseye of this scene with Jesus: God is all and over all.

When we realize that, life simplifies; it streamlines. Each day Jesus offers that perspective—the choice to slow down and choose to render to the world all the worldly things and take up an altogether different citizenship. It permits a person to reciprocate to Jesus the shared sentiment packaged poetically from the lips of fair Juliet:

My bounty is as boundless as the sea,

My love as deep; the more I give to thee,

the more I have, for both are infinite.

Jesus is Lord of all—bullseye.

10. WORSHIP

"Land of the free and the home of the …"

Francis Scott Key could have put about anything next.

Home of the *good*. Or home of the *bright*. He could have been materialistic and gone with home of the *rich*. Or altruistic: home of the *true*. So many things could fit, but the quality he chose to describe himself and his countrymen: Brave.

Brave. Bravery. Courage.

What is it about courage that compels? And what makes us loathe its opposite quality?

No one wants to be a coward. Ever get called a "coward"? It is an insult that will make one cower. The word is thought to derive from the French word for tail, perhaps meaning the way an animal "turns tail" and runs. To be a coward then, etymologically, is to be less than human. An animal. A scared, scampering beast.

Mark 14 has bravery and cowardice as its theme, bookended by two characters epitomizing these respective qualities. The first is a woman at a party.[95] In those times women were to be seen and not heard. They had a low standing in society, a cultural misogyny baked into the bread of daily life. But this woman, unnamed here in Mark, did not let the fear of convention, the rigidity of societal norms, stay her hand. No, she took in that very hand an alabaster jar of costly perfume—likely worth tens of thousands of dollars—and broke it before Jesus, the object of her worship and the breaker of her cultural chains. She was brave. Worship always is. *Brave. Bravery. Courage.* It takes courage to follow, to trust, to try—to stand up and stand out for the beauty of truth.

Peter was at this same party, a follower of Jesus for years by this point in the Jesus narrative. Toward the end of Mark 14, Jesus suggests that his followers would fall away—they would not find the courage to stand firm. Peter argues that "Even if all fall away, I will not."[96] He has words, bravado. But his courage is fleeting—it turns tail and runs. When Jesus is arrested, Peter denies knowing Jesus three times. On that night, he was a coward, the courage of former worship gone simpering and silent.

It is hard to know sometimes if we'll be brave, isn't it? Of course, we all, like Peter, think we will be. Some friends and I were discussing the Holocaust recently—just some light conversation, I know. But the conversation spent a few moments on if we'd be the type of people who would have, at great peril to ourselves, harbored Jewish people in our homes. Of course, we would be heroes. Just ask us.

Some research pertaining to that very quandary suggests that the people who were most likely to protect Jews from the Nazis were those raised with high-risk thresholds and adherence for empathy over rules.[97] Often this was a result of being born later in a family. Later-borns are often compelled to risk more to get attention and could get away with more thanks to over-extended parents. (We've yet to name our youngest. We'll get to it if we can ever find where we left her.) Empathy is often born from relating actions not with hard-and-fast rules but with feelings. So rather than being told as children, "Don't hit!" those who are reprimanded with something like, "How do you think that makes Joseph feel when you hit him?" were far more likely to buck the edicts of the Reich for the whispers of the conscience.[98] Therefore, some predictor of courage is conditioned into our upbringing. Are we rule-followers and first-borns doomed to *peter* out when adversity comes calling?

Let's return to the anthem. Before it is the home of the brave, it is "the land of the free." Maybe there is something in that? That, regardless of upbringing, courage is still a choice. It may be a harder choice for some of us than others, but we can all open our doors—our hidden rooms—to what is right regardless of social and familial conditioning. Whatever our social standing, then, the courage to worship is an option; it is a freedom bestowed. What to do with that freedom remains.

For me, this conjures the Cowardly Lion. The famous character is supposed to be the king of all beasts yet fears his own shadow. In the books, despite this fear, he approaches Dorothy—which goes against his very moniker. He then chronicles his malady to Dorothy, a leap of courageous vulnerability. And off to see the Wizard they go—facing dangers and crossing treacherous chasms along the way.

The Cowardly Lion is terribly afraid but presses on. It is not the sudden absence of fear that moves him onward, but an unrelenting propulsion through it toward the hope of something better. The kinship of his friends and the longing for the Wizard has him roar in inner defiance at his own cowardice. He pushes bravely on, despite expectations or social standing. In freedom, he forges ahead; he breaks an alabaster jar all his own.

In Mark 14, wedged between the worshipful, perfume-pouring woman and the cowering, creeping Peter is a distraught version of Jesus. Sitting in a garden, awaiting his arrest, he laments: "My soul is overwhelmed with sorrow to the point of death." [99]

Here is a troubled man. He looks at the world around him, at the circumstances marching toward him, and it is not an anthem that springs forth, but a dirge. "Father," he prays to God, "everything is possible for you. Take this cup from me. Yet not what I will, but what you will." [100]

He is chronicling his malady, a leap of courageous vulnerability. And in the moments to come, he is arrested, beaten, and nailed to a tree, crossing the treacherous chasm—a propulsion through death for something better.

Mark 14 is a study in courage: in being set free to be brave, even when our souls are overwhelmed to the point of death. We lay our cowardice down and walk on into the storms set before us toward the hope of a collective "something better."

But that is only true if we choose it. Worship is a giving of ourselves as completely as possible, to a hope and a truth that is beyond, to a risky identity that endures scorn, and danger, and ridicule, pain, and even death, for the sake of sacred freedom.

Jesus offers us this. It isn't for the good people or the later-borns or the ones raised the right way. It is for the brave. The ones who will break the jar, pour themselves out, and follow the road, even across deadly chasms. Jesus gives us a courage and then invites us, like him, to use it.

Will you?

The land of the free, the home of the brave, pushing bravely on.

11. DEATH

If we are honest, the death of Jesus isn't that big of a deal because it isn't our death. It is the way we feel when we see a news story depicting a tragedy a world away. Yes, we shake our heads and maybe even say some distraught-sounding words, but we don't cancel our pickleball game. Beyond that, not only is Jesus not us, he's not even in the same time zone, historically speaking. JFK's death is fodder for speculation, entertainment, and even humor. Lincoln, King, Jr., and Kennedy might be the stuff of statues, but the statute of limitations has run out on their deaths producing any kind of grave impact. Like them, Jesus' death's biggest impact is likely to come on trivia night or in meme-making.

My son has this accidentally morbid book about a mouse named Samson who boards the *Titanic*. The goal of the book is apparently to teach toddlers about catastrophes and freezing in the Atlantic. It does a good job. I couldn't believe the first time I read it to him; subsequent readings featured a good deal of censorship, which has the story concluding with a fun swimming party—*They are crying in the water because they are laughing so very hard,* I lie. Many things stand out about the fretful voyage of the *Titanic*, but one is the different perspectives aboard the ship. That mouse in my son's story was pretty confused, and can you blame him? He got cast in a children's book—that usually doesn't end with you also being cast into the Atlantic Ocean. But the real-life people weren't much clearer on the events upon striking the iceberg. On the top deck, for instance, there were three small bumps, not enough to spill the champagne. A snowball fight even broke out. Here's a surviving passenger's recollection of that tragic night:

Just before going to my state room, A11, there was a bump. As I turned the
handle of my room [door], there was another bump. As I got into my room, there
was a third bump … like little pushes, nothing violent … As I got out onto the
promenade deck, I saw a large grey, what looked to me like a building, floating
by. But that "building" kept bumping along the rail, and as it bumped it sliced
off bits of ice [which] fell all over the deck. We just picked up the ice and started
playing snowballs. We thought it was fun. We asked the officers if there was any
danger, and they said, "Oh, no, nothing at all, nothing at all, nothing at all. Just
a mere nothing. We just hit an iceberg."[101]

I imagine if the captain were describing this in one word "fun" wouldn't
make the list. Nor would it show up for those belowdecks, as water rushed
in nearly as fast as the panic. In three hours, regardless of perspective, the
unsinkable *Titanic* was unsinkable no more.

The death of Jesus, similarly, has vantages galore. Mark highlights the
soldiers, for example.[102] They aren't frivolous about it—no snowball fights.
Their squabble is practical in nature—who gets Jesus' clothes? My guess is
that these clothes weren't very nice, so perhaps they were after these for use
on the secondary market? It would be like catching a famous record-setting
home run ball or Tom Brady's last touchdown pass—there could be a huge
re sale value. In their materialism and their vocation, they don't even see
Jesus. He is merely an opportunity for gain and part of the job.

Often, I go through life the same way, especially regarding the story of an
ancient carpenter from somewhere I couldn't point out on a map. They cast
lots for his clothes, and my own lot in life has been cast: to do my work
admirably well and benefit from the comforts diligence affords. Yes, if a
homerun ball of distinction ends up in my lap, all the better. But my life is
about completing what has been set before me. Jesus is, at best, a distraction
and, at worst, a costly one. I have fallen asleep to the pleasantness of the

American dream, and I need no nightmarish tale of sin and death to bestir me from sweet slumber.

Then there is the vantage of the religious leaders.[103] They mock Jesus because they won the day. They had been contending against Jesus for years, pitting their world view against his. Finally, the day of reckoning had arrived, and the world got to compare the religious leaders' work against his: he had nails driven through his hands, while they grinned, hammer in hand.

In most things in life, I'd rather be right and dead than wrong. If Jesus were some sort of god, that would still, for these religious elites, be bad news. Very bad news—it would bankrupt their earning potential. But even worse, it would crash the economy of their ideas. A whole life stacked precipitously upon a rug, well, when someone saunters up and grabs the edges of the rug, protection is all that matters. Like the religious leaders, I know the way to navigate life, *thank you.* I don't need some pretender suggesting some new way to do what I'm capable of handling myself.

Pilate also has a curious angle in that he believes Jesus is innocent. I'm no judge—heck, I can't even get past the first hour when jury duty comes calling—but I'm pretty sure it is counter to *Judge 101* to let the innocent person die a gruesome death. Judge Judy would never. Mark 15:15 gives the reason for Pilate's action (or inaction): "Wanting to satisfy the crowd …."

Might not be a good judge, but Pilate's motive checks out. When I have considered Jesus—his story and claims—that is the prevailing thought. I remember getting preached at as a kid and then having some dude in a white suit, à la Mark Twain, have the band play a hymn. *I surrender all* the lyrics went, over and over again. We may not surrender all, but this old-timey preacher was going to be certain that we'd at least surrender lunch. During those tortuous altar calls, I never once contemplated being moved down the aisle for Jesus. But I spent ample mental energy considering what the kids around me would think of me walking down that aisle. No thanks. That is a social surrender I have no interest in.

There is this one guy mentioned, though. Something was different about him. He was a Roman Centurion. So death was no stranger to him. Jesus would not benefit this man socially or vocationally; the "King of the Jews" had no authority over his sphere of life. Yet this soldier watched how Jesus died and concluded, "Surely this man was the Son of God."

I used to wonder about what this man saw, and why his perspective was so different from so many others in the audience that day—and every day since. Why did he walk that aisle of belief, surrendering all? Specifically, I can't really say I know. I don't know if the man had just lost a child or endured a break-up. Maybe he had committed a crime or lost a bunch of money in a gambling scheme. He may have been a secret addict or some sinister miscreant. He might have just been a guy on a cloudy day. But I think in large part the realization of the man was compelled by Jesus' own prediction: "For even the Son of Man did not come to be served, but to serve, and to give his life as a ransom for many."[104]

If we are honest, the death of Jesus isn't that big of a deal because it isn't our death. For the centurion that day, he realized the death of Jesus is a big deal because it was precisely the centurion's death. Your death. My death.

The trouble with the *Titanic* was obvious on the inside. Below deck, near the breach, it was apparent that things were amiss; the freezing destruction, a dark ocean, was flooding in—it was only a matter of time. Reality was not the decadence above.

Though we hide our sin away, it is flooding in and accumulating and securing for us a death mere hours away. Deep down, don't we all know it? Sitting in that church with that white-suited preacher, I knew he was right. He spoke about misdeeds, and I could hide—I wasn't as bad as some of the kids I knew. But then he went deeper in, talking about the thoughts that lived within: the treacherous envy and bitterness and shame—the lurking, freezing destruction. I may not be a bad guy, but in that moment the vantage was clear—I was certainly a sinful one.

Christianity may be real and it may not be. But it is hard to look on at the life of Jesus, a God who is willing to die my death, and not be a bit staggered. What sort of story has the death of the heroic main character on behalf of a flawed minor one? Well, the best sort of story does.

The death Jesus took from me was upon a cross, a symbol we see worn and tattooed on believers and unbelievers alike. It is because the story of the cross resonates deeply. It strikes the very heart of the ship, and reverberates beyond three harmless bumps; no, instead it is a steady thrumming heartbeat, the essence of life, even amid the onrush of death.

Crosses also adorn the heights. I remember being someplace in the Alps. It was snow-enveloped beauty in every direction, and there, in the distance, at a great height: a cross. I hiked and rolled and climbed and stumbled my way to it. And there in the shadow of the cross I used the restroom on the snow—a picture of humanity if ever there was one. My own fallibility there at the base of something pure. I gazed up at that cross, and then began to focus beyond it, down and out at the village in the valley below—the cross stood before and above it.

Atop churches, too, especially long-standing ones, are crosses. They rest, glinting gold, bedecking the skies above. An above where humans place transcendence, God. Were the wrath of God to come, it would surely rain down from above. But first, it would meet the cross, just as it did on that hill thousands of years ago. The centurion watched as God's wrath was poured out on the sacrificial ransom for many. The ultimate Judge took the ultimate sacrifice so that I might receive the ultimate pardon.

The *Titanic* was short lifeboats. Wooden boats could have saved many lives that fateful night. As the bleakness set in, the band took up their instruments. There, as the ship sank into the abyss of the Atlantic, musicians played a final number. It was an old hymn, and it spoke of a rescue which utilized an altogether different form of wood.[105] The music played that night, with its lyrics surely dancing across the heart of the centurion on that cloudy morning of Jesus' death:

Nearer, my God, to Thee
Nearer to Thee
E'en though it be a cross
That raiseth me.

12. LIFE

Once upon a time, my wife's mother collapsed in a Walgreens; she landed in a coma. Six days later, she was dead. It was a Tuesday, I think—the day she fell. She was at the store running an errand.

At the funeral I did what I have always done when someone dear to me dies. Of course, you mumble the songs that are played and cry or try not to cry. You vacantly listen to the condolences, a steady repetition of hollow reminders and timid well-wishes. But there is always part of me, too, that wills the person lying there to get up. Like Jesus calling Lazarus out of the tomb, you chide and challenge the dearly departed to sit up, to walk, to laugh … to live again. But the person—or former person—just lies there, forever lies there. They'd sneer in mockery at your hopes if death would only let them. But death concedes nothing—what is dead is dead absolutely.

After Jesus dies, some friends go to visit his body, to anoint it per their custom. The question on their minds is: *Who will roll the stone away from the entrance of the tomb?*

Brings to mind the thing Jesus had said, probably within earshot of these women heading to the tomb that day, that faith like a mustard seed could move mountains. A mountain wasn't even in question here, though—these women didn't even have faith enough to roll a stone.

Can't say I blame them. This is death, after all. It is unrelenting. Jesus, in their minds, is very much dead. It is over. Finished.

This had to be a pretty terrible morning for them. Death is a trade—a loved one for a nightmare. The living reality of a living person ceases to be real while a dark figment of unreality becomes fully embodied. Death takes and it takes and it takes. Tale as old as time, until, that is, time stops. And since the beginning, time stops for everyone we love. Eventually, we join the lifeless band, making music no more.

This notion consumes us if we live life honestly. Of course, many of us choose not to live life honestly, instead choosing to hide constantly from the reality of death. We busy ourselves and exercise and eat healthy and pretend that those mortality rates that are a click away are more suggestions than cold, dead facts.

These women may not know the specific data points, but they know death when they see it. It is over. Finished. *Who will roll the stone away from the entrance of the tomb?*

They get their answer: "But when they looked up, they saw the stone, which was very large, had been rolled away."

Jesus changes everything. No longer does he permit the heaviness of a stone to weigh one down. These women hadn't even considered that the departed could sit up, walk, laugh … live again. They focused on the stone because it was a solid depiction of reality—at least, what reality had been. Live—die. Live—die. Live—die. Actually, it is not the pattern old as time because it is the one that is older than time—it is the pattern that established time, for each second is really just a tick toward finale. It is over. Finished.

But then Jesus changes everything. He lived. Then died. Then took up his life anew. Forever.

If the tomb is empty, those who follow Jesus step out of casket, shake death off, and live life differently. Jesus changes how they deal with impending death and present suffering, how they watch the news, how they interact with the world around them. The life Jesus offers has the look of one who knows something others might not; it looks like someone unhindered by the worldly weight imposed on them. It looks like peace that surpasses understanding.

If the tomb is empty, I suffer well.

If the tomb is empty, I choose love over fear.

If the tomb is empty, my hope isn't dependent on some election.

If the tomb is empty, I am free from material things—my joy is no longer tethered to some materialistic dock.

If the tomb is empty, everything will work together for my good— somehow, someway.

If the tomb is empty, death loses its sting.

If the tomb is empty, life lives eternal.

If …

If the tomb is empty.

I spend most of my life asking the wrong questions, worrying about the wrong things. I fixate on the stones of the world because I don't have the fortitude—the faith—to break from the age-old cycle. I prefer an empty existence I understand over an empty tomb I don't.

But maybe an answer is to stop asking so many questions, and rather respond to the one Jesus asks: *Who do you say that I am?*

The essence of the *Gospel of Mark* is that Jesus came in love to live and die for you. And then live again, conquering death for all who would choose something different—an empty tomb. Life. The reverse narrative wherein everything bad comes untrue, forever.

The women reached the tomb and saw that the stone, which was very large, had been rolled away. Their worries went with it. These women came to pay witness to death; they left in search of Life.

If the tomb is empty, I can do the same.

AFTERWORD

I will now ask you to judge this book by its cover. Go on, give it a look. The reason I point it out to you isn't for what is there, but rather what isn't. In the original design, there was a little cross on one of those rolling hills. The ghost of Luther came swooping in, muttering, "The Christian shoemaker does his duty not by putting little crosses on the shoes, but by making good shoes."

"Get lost, ghost!" I replied.

My wife left the room, as she does when my ghosts come out.

But I thought about that little cross a fair bit. The book title already has the name of Jesus in it, yet the temptation for the Christian is to then put up three crosses, unleash some doves, and swim in some ichthyses for good measure. We want to Clark Griswold the lawns of our world view no matter how obnoxiously confusing it is.

The counter to this, of course, is to hide the cross entirely. That is the course I took—it served no aesthetic purpose for this cover. That is also, I fear, the course modern Christianity has taken. Christians of the culture wars, for a time, obsessed over the wretched pagans "taking the Christ out of Christmas." Meanwhile, we same Christians took Christ out of everything else—our relationships, our behaviors, our churches, our gospel, our love for friend and foe alike.

The false choice presents itself: We either feature the cross so nothing else can be seen or we hide the thing away altogether. Either way, the person of Jesus gets lost.

The purpose of this book was simply to attempt to focus on Jesus, and give a snapshot of the way of life he offers. Many base their belief or unbelief in Jesus on a strange youth group experience or religious systems, or on bad followers or creepy priests or historical blunders of the supposed faithful. But Jesus asks, "Who do you say that *I* am?" He is the starting point of belief or unbelief, yet we've left him buried, the lede of his good news buried along with him.

I chose not to include the cross on the cover, but I hope it has been evident on each page. I wish I could have done a better, more loving job of conveying these few encounters with Jesus, but it is like that snippet from Mark 12. There is this poor widow who gives a few copper coins. She, out of her poverty, put in all she had. Meager though it may be, this is my offering. I hope it finds you (and your soul) well.

ENDNOTES

CHAPTER 1

1 D.A. Carson, Douglass Moo, Leon Morris. *An Introduction to the New Testament.* Zondervan, 1992.

2 Jay-Z. "Public Service Announcement." *The Black Album.* New York, 2003.

3 Mark 1:1

4 Mark 1:9

5 Genesis 1:2-3

6 Keller, Timothy. *Jesus the King: Understanding the Life and Death of the Son of God.* Penguin Books, 2013.

7 Genesis 1:3

8 Mark 1:11

CHAPTER 2

9 Loconte, Jospeph. *A Hobbit, A Wardrobe, and a Great War.* Thomas Nelson, 2017.

10 Ibid.

11 Zaleski, Philip Zaleski and Carol. *The Fellowship: THe Literary Lives of the Inklings.* Farrar, Straus and Giroux, 2016.

12 https://en.wikipedia.org/wiki/Sexuality_in_The_Lord_of_the_Rings

13 Trueman, Carl R. *The Rise and Triumph of the Modern Self: Cultural Amnesia, Expressive Individualism, and the Road to Sexual Revolution.* Crossway, 2020.

14 Cole, R. Alan. *The Gospel According to Mark: An Introduction and Commentary.* Eerdmans Publishing Co, 1990.

15 Google seems to think it was a motivational speaker named Jim Rohn.

16 For instance: KJV, ESV, NLT, The Message, etc.

17 Lewis, C.S. *The Four Loves.* HarperOne, 2017.

18 Thoreau, Henry David. *Walden and Civil Disobedience.* Signet, 2012.

19 Brooks, David. *The Second Mountain: The Quest for a Moral Life.* Random House,

2020.

20 Lewis, C.S. *The Four Loves*. HarperOne, 2017.

21 Steinbeck, John. *Of Mice and Men*. Penguin Books, 1993.

22 Bonhoeffer, Dietrich. *Life Together: The Classic Exploration of Christian Community*. HarperOne, 1978.

23 Mark 2:5

CHAPTER 3

24 Greenblatt, Stephen. *Will in the World: How Shakespeare Became Shakespeare*. W.W. Norton & Company, 2016.

25 Leacock, Stephen. *Nonsense Novels*. Dodo Press, 2007.

26 Lewis, C.S. *Mere Christianity*. HarperOne, 2015.

27 Mark 3:23

28 Mark 3:24-29

29 Meatloaf. "I'd Do Anything for Love (But I Won't Do That)." *Bat Out of Hell II: Back Into Hell*. 1993.

30 John 10:10

31 Modest Mouse. "Float On." *Good News for People Who Love Bad News*. 2004.

32 Genesis 9:20-27

33 Keller, Timothy. "The Defeat of Evil." New York: Redeemer Presbyterian Church, 2 April 2006. Sermon.

34 Rowling, J.K. *Harry Potter and the Sorcerer's Stone*. Scholastic, 1998.

CHAPTER 4

35 Greene, Andy. *The Office: The Untold Story of the Greatest Sitcom of the 2000s*. Dutton, 2020.

36 Cole, R. Alan. *The Gospel According to Mark: An Introduction and Commentary*. Eerdmans Publishing Co, 1990.

37 I Kings 9:11-13

38 Chesterton, G.K. *Heretics and Orthodoxy*. Lexham Press, 2017.

39 Lewis, C.S. *The Screwtape Letters*. HarperOne, 2015.

40 Keller, Timothy. "The Defeat of Evil." New York: Redeemer Presbyterian Church, 2 April 2006. Sermon.

41 Song of Solomon 2:15

42 Exodus 16:3, Numbers 14:4

43 Postman, Neil. *Amusing Ourselves to Death*. Penguin Books, 1985.

44 W. H. Auden, "In the Autumn of the Age of Anxiety," *New York Times Magazine*, 8 Aug. 1971, late ed., sec. 6:10.

45 W.H. Auden, "The Means of Grace," review of *The Nature and Destiny of Man*, by Reinhold Niebuhr, *The New Republic*, 2 June 1941, 766.

46 Acuff, Jon. *Soundtracks: The Surprising Solution to Overthinking*. Baker Books, 2021.

CHAPTER 5

47 Mark 10:15, Matthew 19:14

48 Mark 12:29-31

49 Comer, John Mark. *The Ruthless Elimination of Hurry*. WaterBrook, 2019.

CHAPTER 6

50 Stevenson, Robert Louis. *The Strange Case of Dr. Jekyll and Mr. Hyde*. Dover Publications, 1991.

51 Brooks, Arthur C. *From Strength to Strength*. Penguin, 2022.

52 Senior, Jennifer. "Happiness Won't Save You." *The New York Times*. November 24, 2020. https://www.nytimes.com/2020/11/24/opinion/happiness-depression-suicide-psychology.html.

53 Staples, Tim. "Seven Reasons Why Peter is the Rock." *Catholic Answers Magazine*. May 6, 2020. https://www.catholic.com/magazine/online-edition/peter-the-rock.

54 Baron, Robert. *Catholicism: A Journey to the Heart of the Faith*. Image, 2014.

55 The quote is likely apocryphal as to whether Rockefeller formally said "just a little more" or "just one more dollar." Its wide attribution hints at veracity in some form, though the setting is likely exaggerated.

56 Studies abound which put the number between $70,000 to $85,000 in America.

57 Brooks, David. *The Second Mountain: The Quest for a Moral Life*. Random House, 2020.

58 Ecclesiastes 3:11

59 Fitzgerald, F. Scott. *The Great Gatsby*. Scribner, 2004.

60 Keller, Timothy. *The Reason for God: Belief in an Age of Skepticism*. Penguin Books, 2009.

61 Piper, John. "Sacred Schizophrenia." Boyce College Commencement, Louisville,

KY. May 12, 2017. Commencement Address. https://www.desiringgod.org/
messages/sacred-schizophrenia

62 Solzhenitsyn, Aleksandr. *The Gulag Archipelago*. Harper Perennial Modern
Classics, 2007.

63 Philippians 1:6

64 Stark, Rodney. *The Triumph of Christianity: How the Jesus Movement Became the
World's Largest Religion*. New York: HarperOne, 2011.

65 Owen, John. *Overcoming Sin and Temptation: Three Classic Works*. Crossway,
2015.

CHAPTER 7

66 Mumford, Lewis. *Technics and Civilization*. The University of Chicago Press,
2010.

67 Micah 7:19, Hebrews 8:12, Isaiah 43:25

68 Mark 9:5

69 Keller, Timothy. *Jesus the King: Understanding the Life and Death of the Son of
God*. Penguin Books, 2013.

70 Mayer, John. "Something's Missing." *Heavier Things*. Columbia Records, 2003.

71 Winter, Ralph. *Perspectives on the World Christian Movement*. William Carey
Library, 2013.

72 Matthew 22:39

73 Matthew 17:20

CHAPTER 8

74 Mark 11:12-18

75 I John 4:8,16

76 Deuteronomy 20:4, Deuteronomy 3:22, Joshua 23:10

77 Amos 5:24

78 Genesis 1:27

79 Ephesians 4:26

80 Brown video: https://www.youtube.com/watch?v=RZWf2_2L2v8

81 Aristotle. *The Art of Rhetoric*. Penguin Classics, 1992.

82 "Remembering Rosa Parks," PBS Newshour, October 25, 2005, https:www//
www.pbs.org/newshour/show/remembering-rosa-parks.

83 James 1:19

CHAPTER 9

84 Mark 12:13

85 Mark 12:15

86 Mark 12:14

87 Mark 12:15-16

88 Jeremiah 29:5-7

89 The New York Times, June 3, 1982, Section B, Page 14. *nytimes. com/1982/06/03/us/nixon-remark-draws-laugh-from-kennedy.html.*

90 Beaty, Katelyn. *Celebrities for Jesus: How Personas, Platforms, and Profits are Hurting the Church.* Brazos Press, 2022.

91 Philippians 3:20

92 Avett Bros. "Head Full of Doubt, Road Full of Promise." *I and Love and You.* American Records, 2009.

93 I Peter 2:13-17

94 I Corinthians 15:55-57

CHAPTER 10

95 Mark 14:3-9

96 Mark 14:29

97 Samuel P. Oliner and Pearl M. Oliner. *The Altruistic Personality.* Touchstone, 1992.

98 Grant, Adam. *Originals.* Penguin Books, 2017.

99 Mark 14:34

100 Mark 14:36

CHAPTER 11

101 Lord, Walter. *A Night to Remember.* Henry Holt and Company, 2005.

102 Mark 15:24

103 Mark 15:31-32

104 Mark 10:45

105 Christianity Explored. *The Cross.* Christianity Explored Ministries, 2011.

DISCUSSION QUESTIONS

INTRODUCTION

1. What creates the environment for good conversation?

2. Do you find it challenging to discuss faith openly? Why or why not?

3. How have conversations about faith or religion opened or closed you off to the idea of faith or religion?

4. Is discussing faith important? Why or why not?

5. What are some of your thoughts about God/faith/religion?

CHAPTER 1

1. What is the best news you've ever received?

2. Have you ever expected bad news but instead been surprised by good news?

3. What experiences and ideas do you tell people about?

4. What recommendations do you make? Why?

5. How would you describe it?

CHAPTER 2

1. Have you ever had a great friend? If so, what made that friend great?

2. Why does friendship matter? What does it provide for a person?

3. Is friendship a modern priority? Why or why not?

4. How are friendship and faith tied together?

5. Why do the men in the story help the paralytic?

6. Is it true that we favor physical things over spiritual things?

7. Why does Jesus put such an emphasis on the inner being?

CHAPTER 3

1. How do you define family?

2. How can strong belief in something sever familial bonds? How can it unify these bonds?

3. In considering the trilemma of liar, lunatic, or lord, how do you categorize Jesus?

4. Do you agree that family is integral to God's plan for humanity? Why or why not?

5. Who can become part of Jesus' family? Is anyone disallowed from joining this family?

6. What makes a "good" church?

CHAPTER 4

1. Do you believe in good and evil?

2. Can miracles really happen? Why or why not?

3. How do you feel about strange things in the Bible/religion?

4. How do you decide what is good and what is evil?

5. Are there unseen spiritual agents in the world?

6. If you were Satan, how would you aim to destroy you?

7. How can evil become progressive or systemic? Can you think of any examples?

8. On what trajectory are the behaviors and ideas in your life taking you?

CHAPTER 5

1. What does rest mean to you?

2. How do you structure your life in a way that minimizes rest?

3. Do you know anyone whose pace of life you admire? Why?

4. How do/might you wrench rest into your regular rhythms? How do/could you Sabbath?

5. Is the idea of God resting strange to you?

6. What would it take for you to have a more peaceful life?

7. What is your functional relationship with time and the concept of eternity?

8. Do you actively invite quiet into your life?

CHAPTER 6

1. How do you view humans: good? Bad? Some mixture?

2. What is the Hedonic Treadmill? What creates for you a treadmill existence?

3. Four idols are mentioned: money, power, pleasure, and fame. Have any of these ever had a grip on facets of your life?

4. How does one avoid an objectified life?

5. Why do Christians do bad things?

CHAPTER 7

1. Jesus asks, "Who do you say I am?" How do you answer that question? Why?

2. What limits your belief in Jesus? What, if anything, activates that belief?

3. Do you think you are sinner? Why or why not?

4. What is the point of religion? How might that differ from faith?

5. Do you think religion is difficult? Why or why not?

6. What is the difference between honest and dishonest doubt?

7. What is Jesus' approach to religion? What about faith?

8. Have you ever felt like something was missing in life?

9. Is perfect faith possible? Is it required?

10. How can one battle unbelief?

CHAPTER 8

1. What makes you angry?

2. Is anger good or bad?

3. What are healthy ways of dealing with anger?

4. How do you manage strong feelings/emotions?

5. What stands out to you about Jesus' anger?

6. Have you ever written a prayer/meditation for your anger? If you did, what would be important for you to include?

7. What things can create barriers to faith—for you and others? How can anger be a barrier?

8. Are there any ways in which you could be released through forgiveness?

9. In a culture of offense, how might you be a peacemaker?

CHAPTER 9

1. Why are humans drawn to stories?

2. What makes a great story?

3. What does it mean to be a good citizen? Do you think this is an expectation of faith or not?

4. How is power a paradox?

5. In what ways does modern church mirror culture?

6. What is so alluring about the idea of celebrity?

7. How might being a citizen of heaven be a liberating paradigm?

CHAPTER 10

1. What is courage? Where have you seen it displayed?

2. Do you go all-in on anything in your life? Why or why not?

3. What do you worship? Why?

4. How is worship an act of courage?

CHAPTER 11

1. How does the story and death of Jesus grow stale?

2. In what ways are our outer lives and inner lives mismatched?

3. What, in life, determines our perspective? What do you find yourself focusing on day-to-day and year-to-year?

4. How much do what people think determine your choices, beliefs, and behaviors?

5. What does the death of Jesus accomplish?

CHAPTER 12

1. How do you think about death?

2. Regardless of belief, is the Jesus resurrection narrative compelling to you? Why or why not?

3. What stands out to you about the life, words, and story of Jesus?

4. Why is it difficult to talk openly about faith/religion/Jesus?

5. If Jesus is real and you could ask him one question, what would it be?

6. If Mark's account is true about Jesus, how do you answer Jesus' question: *Who do you say that I am?*

www.ingramcontent.com/pod-product-compliance
Lightning Source LLC
Chambersburg PA
CBHW020251130626
46549CB00005B/2176